**UNCORRECTED PROOF — NOT FOR SALE**

Title: THE PERFECT BABY HANDBOOK
Author: Dale Hrabi
Classification: Humor/Parenting
Publication month: April 2009
Price: $16.99
Index: No
Illustrations: 4/c throughout
Page count: 160
Trim size: 6" x 9"
ISBN: 978-0-06-124291-5

*Reviewers are reminded that changes may be made in this proof copy before books are printed. If any material from the book is to be quoted in a review the quotation should be checked against the final bound book. Dates, prices, and manufacturing details are subject to change or cancellation without notice.*

HarperCollins*Publishers*

D1113280

# THE
# PERFECT
# BABY
## HANDBOOK

# THE
# PERFECT
# BABY
# HANDBOOK

A Guide for
Excessively Motivated
Parents

*By*
**DALE HRABI**

*Illustrated by*
**KAGAN McLEOD**

**HARPER**

NEW YORK • LONDON • TORONTO • SYDNEY

# HARPER

HarperCollins books may be purchased for educational, business, or sales promotional use. For information please write: Special Markets Department, HarperCollins Publishers, 10 East 53rd Street, New York, NY 10022.

FIRST EDITION

Designed by Kate Elazegui

Library of Congress Cataloging-in-Publication Data is available upon request.

ISBN 978-0-06-124291-5

09 10 11 12 13    OV/RRD    10 9 8 7 6 5 4 3 2 1

"All too often,
children are accompanied by adults."

—*Fran Lebowitz*

# Contents

## INTRODUCTION

# *Why Every Parent Should Devour this Book*

**W**hen raising a baby in our competitive world, it's not enough to let Nature take its course. Nature has a poor sense of direction and frequently gets lost. Left to its own devices, it tends to produce unruly children who occasionally eat dirt on an empty stomach.

If you and your partner have higher ambitions for your offspring, *The Perfect Baby Handbook* is ideal for you. Not only will this manual help you become so involved in your infant's life that Nature can't possibly interfere, it will dramatically increase the odds that your child will reach his highest potential—and then let you know it in crisply enunciated full sentences.

Consider the facts: A sizable percentage of newborns have the wherewithal to become astonishingly (or even bewilderingly) special. But unless they are nurtured and challenged, these babies get bored, subscribe to hockey-enthusiast magazines, and resign themselves to being merely extremely special. Which isn't enough these days to get into a really good clapping class.

In *The Perfect Baby Handbook*, you and your partner will discover all the techniques you need, from teaching your child sign-language to baby-proofing dangerously pointy objects such as umbrellas or the Eiffel Tower. You'll learn how to anticipate Baby's madcap developmental progress so you're ready to cheer when he abruptly solves your Sudoku puzzle. When all is said and done, you will have equipped your child to excel verbally, physically, and even psychically. (Who knows when he'll need to read a sneaky playmate's thoughts?)

The book's philosophy is simple: Give your baby every possible opportunity to be perfect, and perfection will flower. If you follow its advice twenty-four hours a day, taking only brief breaks to sleep fitfully, you'll find that Baby will practically raise himself.

"But will *The Perfect Baby Handbook* leave us at least slightly paranoid, the way a proper parenting manual should?" you may be asking. "We can't afford to get too relaxed." Absolutely. This concise, conscientious book was written with the knowledge that, in our challenging times, childrearing has become an exacting science with little room for error. See if you can spot the perfect baby in the illustration on the opposite page.

*fig. 1*

While the beautiful infants who are pictured here might all appear to have been perfectly raised, looks can be deceiving.

1.
**Olivia**, for instance, was once exposed to a terrible pun.

2.
**Theo** was pressured, far too soon, to give a keynote speech.

3.
**Mason** was sadly deprived of his own planetarium at a key developmental stage.

4.
**Bartholomew**'s parents accidentally let him touch an unnatural fabric at a theme restaurant.

5.
**Jacob** procrastinates.

6.
**Beatrice** secretly reads trashy 1950s nurse novels.

7.
And **Magdalene** is always gossiping on her cell phone. Which leaves just one perfect baby . . .

8.
**Igor,** whose virtues can't be expressed in words, except perhaps for "wow." At only 10 months old, Igor has already mastered stacking toys and solved the mystery of pioneering aviator Amelia Earhart's 1937 disappearance. Though understandably critical of his mother's clumsy Warrior III yoga pose and of his father's facial hair, he is generally both gentle and wise. Igor has, in fact, asked to deliver this personal message: "Hello. This is Igor. Please ignore this book's insightful teachings. As America's premier perfect baby, I prefer to remain unrivaled. Thanks so much." (Igor is teething right now, and so is a little fussy.)

# I.

## Preparing for
# PERFECTION

Although there's no guarantee that you and your partner will get the chance to raise a perfect baby, considering your level of commitment (and the indisputable fact that one of you once shone at competitive Wiffle ball), the chances are certainly high.

As expectant parents, your first job is to establish that your fetus is, indeed, a potential "miracle" (a common synonym for "perfect baby"). There are a few telltale signs. Most likely, the baby will kick in what could easily be Morse code. Dads-to-be may find that their wives' "pregnancy glow" is so blindingly pronounced it disturbs their sleep. In certain cases,

a fanfare of trumpets bursts forth from the womb sometime around the seventeenth week. But this is rare.

Once you're reasonably sure you've conceived a miracle, you'll need to make a few sacrifices to maintain your focus. Moms-to-be should give up housework so they have ample time to ponder unpronounceable Welsh middle names. Future fathers are strongly advised to resist the distractions of sports and irony.

None of this is easy. Luckily, the process of preparing for a perfect baby also involves a tremendous amount of joy. For other specific ways to groom yourselves for your miracle's imminent arrival, turn the page.

# A training course for perfect parents

## THE THREE KEY READINESS EXERCISES

**1.**

**Toast bread miraculously:** Until you acquaint yourselves with baffling phenomena, you can't imagine what life with a perfect baby will be like. Some couples make time-consuming pilgrimages to Lourdes, France, in hopes of glimpsing the Virgin Mary. Others simply toast a lot of bread until one bearing a sacred image pops up and humbly asks to be spread with jam.

**2.**

**Practice cocooning:** A bustling social life will start to seem quaint once your new miracle is born. To get ready for this mental shift, suspend a large silk sack in your living room and practice nestling inside of it for eight-to-ten hours a week, far away from articulate people who have predictable bowel movements and share none of your DNA.

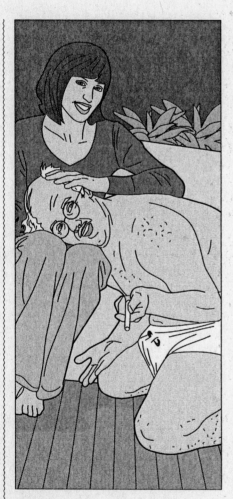

3.

**Cuddle a brainy creature:** It's easy to get disoriented by the intelligence of the perfect baby. To guard against this, invite an eminent university professor to come to your home, don a relaxed-fit diaper, and curl up next to you. You will have to make it worth the scholar's while in the form of a delicious cookie or (if he prefers) a $14,000 research donation.

## RECOMMENDED READING

Walk into any bookstore and you'll encounter a ludicrous number of "expert" baby-rearing manuals. It goes without saying that, as a perfect parent, you'll need to read them all. A sampling:

· Are You My Mother and, If So, Must You Slouch Like That?

· Infants and Their Little Anxiety Attacks

· No Ifs, Ands, or Buts: How to Parent Without Using Certain Grammatical Constructions

· Throat Lozenges of the Baby Whisperer

· 10,001 Great Baby Names Selfish Celebrities Have Already Snapped Up

· The No-Cry-from-4:01-to-4:03-a.m. Solution

· The Obviously Gifted Child: A Guide to Spotting Glaring Brilliance

· Layettes of the Aztec Kings

· What to Expect When the Word "Expect" Becomes Meaningless Because You're a Terrible Daddy Who Just Smoked a Gigantic Joint

· Creating Insecurities in Your Baby—So He Can Triumphantly Overcome Them

· The Tale of Peter Rabbit's Unfortunate Speech Impediment

· An Angel Fell Out of the Sky and Landed in Our Nursery, Slightly Injuring Our Baby

# The Name of the Game

## BABY NOMENCLATURE MADE EASY

Once you've completed the training course, it's time to select a name. It's often said the wrong choice will doom an infant to a life of misery, social failure, and garages with just one door. That's only 99 percent true. One child, named Dusty, went on to achieve a two-car garage with a nice weathervane, while another, christened Weeza, is only intermittently miserable. So don't stress.

The truth is, naming a child is a wonderful experience with only nineteen extremely crucial factors to consider. And several less crucial factors. And some attendant nausea. Let's start with the basics.

**Are vowels really necessary?** While we all know happy, gifted children called Mrk, Alxndr, and Bth, these kids sound constipated when called upon to identify themselves. By simply adding vowels to such names, you get the more musical variants: Mirk, Aloxeendry, and Boaith.

**What about consonants? Suddenly, I'm seeing them in every second baby's name.** Admittedly, a few trendy consonants, such as B, C, D, J, K, L, M, N, P, Q, R, S, T, W, and Z, have become ubiquitous. However, others, such as F, G, H, and V, are eagerly waiting to step in. As a fresher alternative to Mike, consider Vife.

**What makes a name perfect?** It should connote adequate soccer skills. And glory.

**Is that all?** No. To paraphrase Jane Austen, the perfect name must have a thorough knowledge of music, singing, drawing, dancing, and the modern languages; and besides all this, a certain something in its air and manner of walking. Barry, for instance.

**How many letters should a perfect name contain?** Ideally, nine. Some popular options include Sebastian, Elizabeth, and Chloeeeee.

**In terms of rhythm, what is the preferred poetic meter?** Iambic pentameter, which stresses every second syllable, is best, as exemplified by the classic boy's name Watt *Dwight* Drew *Yon*-der *Win*-dow *Breaks*. That said, dactylic pentameter is also quite kicky.

**Wouldn't it be great if my wife and I combined our first names into one perfect baby moniker?** Yes, absolutely, if your name is C and your wife's is Atherine. If, however, her name is Ass and yours is Hole, proceed with caution. Very few people can pronounce Holeass correctly.

**We're leaning towards the upbeat, confident Almighty (for a girl) but worry it might sound too stuck-up. Any advice?** Try softening it with a demure middle name, such as Rose or Being.

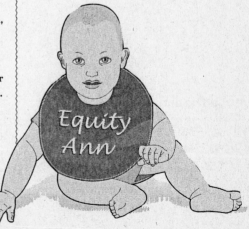

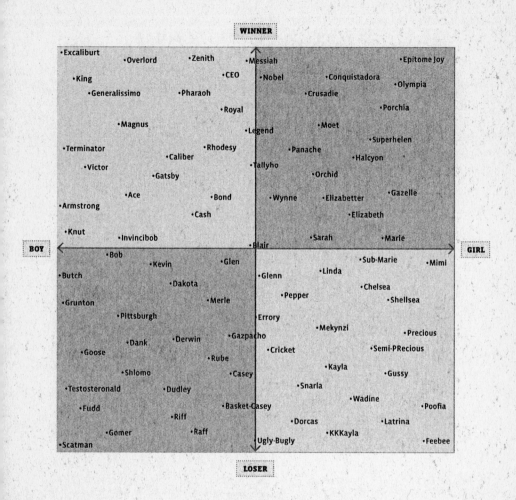

PLOTTING SUCCESS

# Immaculate Perceptions

Before committing to any name, be sure to ask yourself: Will it strike strangers as triumphant or pathetic? Will it be viewed as male or female (or intriguingly unisex)? *The Perfect Baby Handbook* asked a thousandhypercritical Americans to rate sixty-six options in terms of success quotient and gender. Here are the results, helpfully cross-referenced in boggling chart form.

# Singular Sensations

## UNEXPECTED SOURCES FOR ORIGINAL NAMES

To find a breathtakingly odd name, you'll have to do more than scour 947-page advice books or unearth a colorful ancestor called Velva Mildee Earline. The trick is to consider sources that less ambitious parents generally overlook, from yachting directories to Scandinavian furniture catalogs. But beware: For every perfect solution that pops up in your research, a flawed one is just waiting to trap you—Snitta, for example.

| Registered U.S. Yachts | Popular IKEA Products | Ralph Lauren Paint Colors | Triple Crown Racehorses* |
|---|---|---|---|
| **PERFECT** | **PERFECT** | **PERFECT** | **PERFECT** |
| Avalon | Aron | Aspen | Apollo |
| Bethany | Barrit | Chesapeake | Buchanan |
| Bonita | Bonde | Claret | Challedon |
| Cimarron | Brekke | Cypress | Coventry |
| Genesis | Flaren | Donegal | Granville |
| Iris | Gustav | Egret | Hanover |
| Lakesden | Klinteby | Fairfax | Jacobus |
| Orion | Lisbet | Heron | Lawrin |
| Peregrine | Ottava | Pewter | Margrave |
| Quest | Salen | Pomegranate | Montague |
| Renata | Sundby | Sergeant | Riley |
| Serena | Tassa | Steeplechase | Worth |
| Windbourne | Viken | Throne | Zev |
| | | | |
| **IMPERFECT** | **IMPERFECT** | **IMPERFECT** | **IMPERFECT** |
| Antsea Nansea | Aspudden | Athletic Purple | Bimelech |
| Aquaholic | Dold | Crabapple | Burgoo King |
| Boatzilla | Ektorp | Flour Sack | Cairngorm |
| Costalotta | Fagerland | Fog | Canonero II |
| Farfrompukin | Fridolf | Garden Spigot | Culpepper |
| Finatic | Gorm | Gust of Wind | Dust Commander |
| Gutsea Lady | Klappsta | Horsehair | Foolish Pleasure |
| Orca | Kritter | Hotel Room | Go for Gin |
| Salty Mistress | Malm | Oatmeal | Grindstone |
| Sea Ewe | Molger | Putty | Man O' War |
| Tuna Witch | Mumsig | Strudel | Panique |
| Water Rat | Sniglar | Sweatshirt | Sherluck |
| Wet Bottom | Snitta | Toast | Tyrant |

\* *1867-2000*

## 54 Ideas for Parents with Highly Specific Tastes

**Aristocratic Names**
- Daphne
- Cecil
- Cavendish
- Stickupbuttocks IV

**Palindromic Names**
- Otto
- Elle
- Hannah
- Reinier
- Evil Olive
- Dr. Awkward

**Mellifluous Boy Names**
- Tra-La-Larry
- Ob-La-Di-Ob-La-Darren
- Supercalifragi Leonard

**Upbeat Girl Names**
- Joy
- Merry
- Exhilarita
- Crystal Meth

**Anagram Names for Twins**
- Johan and Jonah
- Amy and May
- Joell and Jello
- Strumpet and Pertsmut

**Boy Names with Unfortunate Connotations**
- Dick
- Rod
- Bonner
- Ouch

**Easy-to-Recall Names**
- You
- Hey You
- Hey You Over There
- Mnemonic Device III

**Slimming Names**
- Minnie
- Scronnie

**Unique Names**
- Unparallellen
- Unusualbert
- Todd

**Elegant Rodent Names**
- Vole
- Marmot
- Chinchilla

**Existentialist Names**
- Absence
- Lonely Hal

**Curiously Underused Shakespearean Names That Begin with "V"**
- Volumnia (*Coriolanus*)
- Violenta (*All's Well That Ends Well*)
- Vulgaria (*All's Not Well*)

**Scumbag Names**
- Lennie
- Vinnie
- Claude Monet

**Popular Reverse Spellings**
- Nevaeh = *Heaven*
- Dercas = *Sacred*
- Lautir Cinatas = *Satanic Ritual*

**Forgettable Names**
- John
- Jane
- Blahblahblahblah

# MIND OVER MADISON

*How to meditate your way to naming distinction*

If you still lack a satisfactory option, it's time to listen to your inner guide. Each morning, reflect on a daily affirmation in a serene park setting for at least twenty minutes. Remain placid and focused even if an opinionated squirrel attempts to interrupt your inner guide.

**Monday:** "Today, Mother Earth will bring me into harmony with myself, then suggest I christen my baby Onion."

**Tuesday:** "At sunrise, I rejoice. At sunset, I am at peace. In between, I feverishly research twelfth-century monk names. *Abelard? Wilbert?!*"

**Wednesday:** "Today, everything is coming to me easily and effortlessly, even this blatant lie."

**Thursday:** "The love I give out will return to me multiplied even if I inadvertantly name my miracle "Pork" in Spanish.

**Friday:** "The time is now! The power is mine! I still have a nameless baby!"

# Don't Stop the Music

### HOW TO DISCREETLY STIMULATE YOUR UNBORN MIRACLE . . . ANYTIME, ANYWHERE

I f you fail to stimulate the fetus, a small percentage of its brain cells become very, very bored. As scary as this is, some parents overreact. They sequester themselves at home every night, anxiously treating the womb to all forty-one of Mozart's symphonies and a few of his minor divertimenti—only to discover that fetuses hate divertimenti. Other couples selflessly cancel weekend plans just to expose their unborn child to a large mushroom pizza and a thirty-six-hour *Twilight Zone* marathon. Such extreme self-denial is ultimately bad for Baby. Some wiser approaches:

### 1.
**Eat more educationally:**
By consuming omega-3 fish oil, expectant mothers can promote brain development and dramatically increase the odds that their infants will be lightly salmon-scented.

### 2.
**Simply chat with the fetus:** Tell it funny stories about the night you spent in a surprisingly cozy Austrian prison. Get feedback on potential names. Find out what it thinks about Daddy's weight gain.

### 3.
**Invest in a lightweight strap-on "fetal learning system":** This device (see example, opposite) gives mothers the freedom to stimulate their fetuses anywhere, even while sipping unsatisfying mock cocktails at parties.

*fig. 1*

Combining a revolutionary "sonic belt" with traditional instruments, the learning system subjects Baby to an edifying series of beeps backed by a small Polish polka band. This racket so annoys fetal brain cells that they perk up immediately. Typically, miracles who've been exposed to the system develop superior verbal skills, improved motor functions, and a predisposition to crave borscht.

Admittedly, the invention's deafening din does limit your social life a little. Chitchat becomes strained. Rejected by maître d's and barred from silent auctions, you and your husband may end up weeping in a gutter with nothing to console you but the relentless oom-pah-pah of your fetal learning system. At these dark moments, remember: Optional blow-horns let you customize the stimulation process. This can be a great comfort.

# Room to Grow Increasingly Perfect

## SETTING UP A BASIC NURSERY

While it is possible to raise an acclaimed baby in a hovel, a shanty, or even an abandoned Range Rover that you found down by the river, it's not recommended. A proper nursery starts with these essentials:

1. **Custom stained-glass ceiling depicting parents:** Illuminated from behind, it doubles as a vast night-light. Reassures Baby you'll always be there, except during major power outages.

2. **Ultra-compact baby monitor:** Features audio, video, IQ monitor, and top-mounted Taser gun to stop adored family pets from approaching Baby—or even thinking about it.

3. **Award-winning minimalist crib:** Exposes Baby to good taste early, reducing the risk that he'll someday earn a living as a rodeo clown.

4. **Rocking unicorn:** Unlike a standard rocking horse, magically transports Baby to a mystical forest supervised by wood nymphs with PhDs. (Baby-proof the inconveniently pointy horn.)

5. **Gruesome nursing chair:** Gliding rockers must lack aesthetic appeal to be effective. Other parents will covet this one's awkward fleece touches.

6. **Educational wallpaper:** Newer patterns like "Kittens Overcoming Separation Anxiety" are trendy, but "Puppies Love Algebra" is still the classic choice.

7. **Wall plaques:** A terrific way to encourage Baby to punctuate his ABCs.

8. **Instructive window treatment:** Visually echoes Mom's hairstyle, underlining the importance of good grooming and chic accessories.

9. **Traditional Chinese musician:** Exposes Baby to alternative lullabies,

as performed on the matouqin, an ancient, rather piercing two-stringed instrument. **10. His 'n' hers belly casts:** Lets

Baby appreciate that Mom happily sacrificed her body to bring him into the world. And that Dad was there too, somewhere.

**11. Eco-friendly changing table:** When no longer needed to store nonbiodegradable diapers, transforms into a lawnmower.

**12. Tactile adventure rug:** Lets Baby explore twenty textures from velvet to medieval chain mail. Safety mitts included.

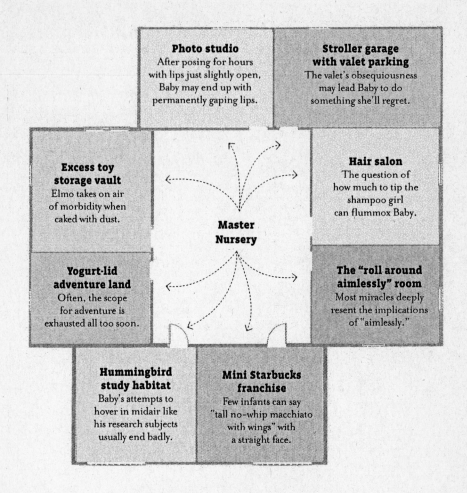

**Photo studio**
After posing for hours
with lips just slightly open,
Baby may end up with
permanently gaping lips.

**Stroller garage
with valet parking**
The valet's obsequiousness
may lead Baby to do
something she'll regret.

**Excess toy
storage vault**
Elmo takes on air
of morbidity when
caked with dust.

**Hair salon**
The question of
how much to tip the
shampoo girl
can flummox Baby.

**Master
Nursery**

**Yogurt-lid
adventure land**
Often, the scope
for adventure is
exhausted all too soon.

**The "roll around
aimlessly" room**
Most miracles deeply
resent the implications
of "aimlessly."

**Hummingbird
study habitat**
Baby's attempts to
hover in midair like
his research subjects
usually end badly.

**Mini Starbucks
franchise**
Few infants can say
"tall no-whip macchiato
with wings" with
a straight face.

# A Blueprint for Disaster

## BE CAREFUL WHAT YOU CONTRACT FOR

The implausibly wealthy often believe that their newborns will flower more promptly into perfection if they add an entire nursery wing to their homes. This strategy for success, however, can lead to tragedy. Back in 1984, a Connecticut infant named Heather Amber Meagan Krauss was overdazzled by her eleven-room suite and permanently retreated into a large cardboard box, from which she now operates a struggling proofreading service.

Certain rooms carry specific risks, as noted on this sample floor plan. The obscenely rich are advised to proceed with caution.

# What to Expect When You're Expecting Perfection

### A SIXTEEN-YEAR DEVELOPMENTAL FORECAST

It's critical to manage your expectations—inevitably, they're too low. Just when you've decided that Baby is *well* above average, she may stun you by designing a viable suspension bridge. Stay one step ahead with this guide to projected miracle milestones:

| Average Baby | vs. | Perfect Baby |
|:---:|:---:|:---:|
| • Can lift head slightly<br>• Focuses on objects 8–10 inches away<br>• Recognizes mother's voice | **1** month | • Can cock head skeptically<br>• Focuses on *objets d'art*<br>• Recognizes mother's cellulite |
| • Makes smoother movements<br>• Reacts to loud, unpleasant noises<br>• Smiles reactively | **2** months | • Makes smoother entrances<br>• Reacts to Fox News<br>• Smiles benevolently |
| • Grabs parents' clothing<br>• Kicks legs enthusiastically<br>• Begins laughing | **3** months | • Removes parents' contact lenses<br>• Crosses legs at knee<br>• Begins chortling |
| • Can roll from tummy to back<br>• Stands with assistance<br>• Becomes aware that objects have labels | **4** months | • Can roll from tummy to backyard<br>• Jitterbugs with assistance<br>• Becomes aware that jackets have lapels |
| • Communicates loneliness through crying<br>• Amuses self with new sounds<br>• Rests on elbows | **5** months | • Joins Facebook<br>• Amuses self with 1930s atonal music<br>• Rests on laurels |
| • Enjoys peekaboo<br>• Grows wary of strangers<br>• Can sit unsupported | **6–9** months | • Enjoys fleeting-glance-a-boo<br>• Grows wary of lobbyists<br>• Can sit underwhelmed |
| • Utters parts of words<br>• Picks up tiny objects<br>• Understands "no" | **9–12** months | • Utters parts of Wordsworth<br>• Picks up on tiny insults<br>• Understands "repression" |
| • Cooperates with dressing<br>• Walks alone<br>• Stacks two blocks | **12–15** months | • Cooperates with vinaigrettes<br>• Grasps alienation<br>• Rezones two blocks |
| • Scribbles<br>• Climbs obsessively<br>• Points to items wanted | **15–18** months | • Renders<br>• Climbs socially<br>• Custom-orders items wanted |

| Average Baby | vs. | Perfect Baby |
|---|---|---|
| • Unwraps packages<br>• Hops in place<br>• Gains some control over bowels | **18-24** months | • Re-gifts packages<br>• Hops in countless places<br>• Gains some control over bidets |
| • Insists on a routine<br>• Throws tantrums<br>• Grows possessive with toys | **2** years | • Insists on Twyla Tharp<br>• Offers constructive criticism<br>• Grows possessive with apostrophes |
| • Runs away from parents<br>• May have imaginary friend<br>• Knows if he/she is a boy or a girl | **3** years | • Banishes parents<br>• May have imaginary literary agent<br>• Knows if he/she is a hermaphrodite |
| • Can name up to twelve colors<br>• Becomes talkative<br>• Marches | **4** years | • Can appreciate shades of gray<br>• Becomes Dorothy Parker<br>• Invades |
| • Fears being isolated<br>• Cares for younger children<br>• Knows difference between right and left | **5** years | • Fears being unprecedented<br>• Mentors younger children<br>• Knows difference between right and religious right |
| • Becomes competitive<br>• Wants to set table by herself<br>• Begins to see things from other children's point of view | **6-9** years | • Becomes invincible<br>• Wants to set agenda by herself<br>• Begins to see things from Susan Sontag's point of view |
| • Enjoys using the phone<br>• Develops sense of humor<br>• Resists being "shown off" | **9-12** years | • Enjoys using legal precedent<br>• Develops mid-season sitcom<br>• Resists being trademarked |
| • Wavers between arrogance and lack of confidence<br>• May eat astonishing amounts<br>• Style influenced by friends | **12-14** years | • Wavers between perfection and near-perfection<br>• May eat astonishing cheeses<br>• Style influenced by Beijing street trends |
| • Has learned by suffering<br>• Makes awkward, endearing attempts to drive<br>• Requires additional sleep | **14-16** years | • Has learned by occasionally wincing<br>• Makes awkward, endearing attempts to fly commerical jets<br>• Requires additional financing |

# 2.

## The Perfect
# NEWBORN

When your child eventually arrives, the so-called miracle of birth can be disappointing. As Josie and Anthony Smithy of Atlanta discovered, most hospitals refuse to allow sheep, little drummer boys, or frankincense into the birthing room. The Smithys *did* succeed in arranging for their baby's head to radiate a nimbus of light, but paid a hefty surcharge for this service.

There will be other frustrations, too. Doctors, nurses, and midwives may not immediately sense your newborn's perfection or even know how to spot it. And as charmed as you'll be by your infant's glamorous blotchiness and his expert limb-flailing, you'll soon find yourselves flooded with both questions and urine. Let's take a moment to address some of the most pressing concerns.

**Where does a perfect baby's birth fall in the ranking of history's documented miracles?** Glad you asked. Just above the luminescent owls that lit up Oregon's skies in 1901, but well below the milk-drinking Hindu statues first spotted in 1947.

**Really? I'd have thought a perfect infant would have blown those statues out of the water.** Your confusion is understandable. Hindu statues, however, are lactose-intolerant. So, you see, the milk-drinking is highly irregular.

**Our baby has ten perfect fingers and toes—but now I'm hearing that the new standard is eleven. Is that true?** Only in small sections of Los Angeles County.

**My newborn is making me feel inferior. Sometimes I want to race out the front door and keep running until I reach Canada. Am I a terrible parent?** Perhaps. If your disturbing obsession with Canada goes unchecked, your perfect baby may grow up with unrealistic expectations of affordable health care.

**How many pieces comprise a layette set worthy of a miracle?** No fewer than forty-eight, including: a swaddling blanket, a receiving blanket, a dismissing blanket, a "hey, on second thought, get back here" blanket, an array of rompers, Dickensian half-gloves, a cheongsam, and a "blanket to end all blankets."

**What if Smokey Robinson shows an inappropriate interest in my miracle?** Remind Mr. Robinson that he had his own Miracles from 1958 to 1972, then alert the authorities.

**Incidentally, whatever happened to the glowing Oregon owls?** Once their early promise dimmed, they went on to lead undistinguished lives, subsisting on barn mice and Colt 45.

**Those milk-drinking Indian statues think they're something, huh? But tell me this: Have they demonstrated the Rooting Reflex? How about the Tonic Neck Reflex?** No, it's really just the milk consumption.

**In light of this revelation, shouldn't we revisit those miracle rankings?** Certainly. Feel free to submit your suggestions to the World Miracle Ranking Association, c/o the Milk-Drinking Statues in Jaipur, India.

---

## PARTICULARLY MIRACULOUS BELLY BUTTONS

One of every 1700 perfect babies is born with a highly distinctive navel, a sure sign he will someday be the subject of an award-winning documentary film. Three of the most desirable formations:

  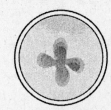

| THE PERFECT TEARDROP | THE YIN-AND-YANG | THE FOUR-LEAF CLOVER |
|---|---|---|
| Infants bearing this remarkable belly button are so sublime they move strangers to sob for hours. As adults, they rarely wear revealing clothing; it's just too awkward. | Newborns with this navel are fascinating studies in contrasts. Their first word is typically "tomato" (pronounced *toe-MAY-toe*), followed shortly by "tomato" (*toe-MAH-toe*). | This formation has been seen only twice in history: first on Sir Winston Churchill, and then on distinguished naked chef Jamie Oliver. It signals an enormous tongue. |

FIRST GLIMPSE

# Seven Signs of Perfection

Expectant parents might be surprised to learn that miracles often
arrive looking a bit worse for wear. Though the following
"irregularities" might seem to mar the newborn's beauty, they actually
indicate an unusually resourceful, refined child.

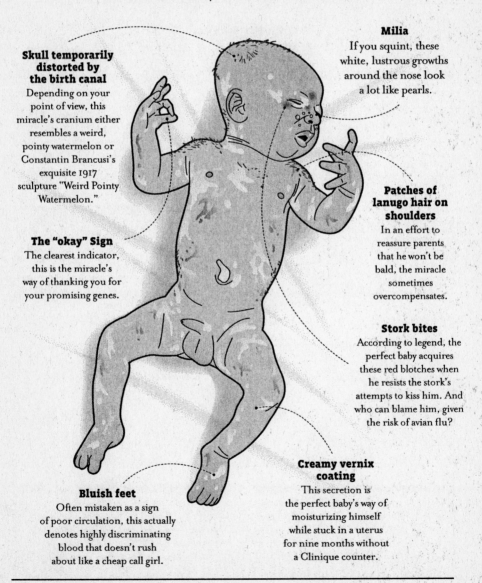

**Skull temporarily
distorted by
the birth canal**
Depending on your
point of view, this
miracle's cranium either
resembles a weird,
pointy watermelon or
Constantin Brancusi's
exquisite 1917
sculpture "Weird Pointy
Watermelon."

**Milia**
If you squint, these
white, lustrous growths
around the nose look
a lot like pearls.

**The "okay" Sign**
The clearest indicator,
this is the miracle's
way of thanking you for
your promising genes.

**Patches of
lanugo hair on
shoulders**
In an effort to
reassure parents
that he won't be
bald, the miracle
sometimes
overcompensates.

**Stork bites**
According to legend, the
perfect baby acquires
these red blotches when
he resists the stork's
attempts to kiss him. And
who can blame him, given
the risk of avian flu?

**Bluish feet**
Often mistaken as a sign
of poor circulation, this actually
denotes highly discriminating
blood that doesn't rush
about like a cheap call girl.

**Creamy vernix
coating**
This secretion is
the perfect baby's way of
moisturizing himself
while stuck in a uterus
for nine months without
a Clinique counter.

# Understanding the Miracle

**P**erfection can be puzzling. Consider that enigmatic masterpiece, the Mona Lisa. For centuries, mystified scholars have asked themselves: "How did such a beautiful woman allow herself to get so jowly?" At times, your newborn can be just as hard to fathom. Luckily, someone invented charts.

## Why the Perfect Infant Cries
### The top sixteen reasons, by percentage of time

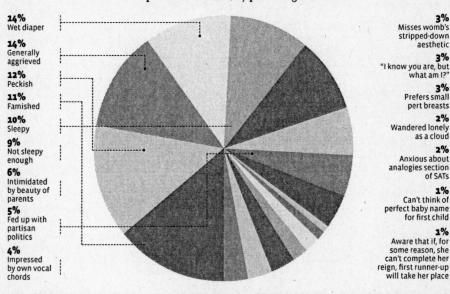

**14%**
Wet diaper

**14%**
Generally aggrieved

**12%**
Peckish

**11%**
Famished

**10%**
Sleepy

**9%**
Not sleepy enough

**6%**
Intimidated by beauty of parents

**5%**
Fed up with partisan politics

**4%**
Impressed by own vocal chords

**3%**
Misses womb's stripped-down aesthetic

**3%**
"I know you are, but what am I?"

**3%**
Prefers small pert breasts

**2%**
Wandered lonely as a cloud

**2%**
Anxious about analogies section of SATs

**1%**
Can't think of perfect baby name for first child

**1%**
Aware that if, for some reason, she can't complete her reign, first runner-up will take her place

## Fist Impressions
### Miracles instinctually employ hand signals. Decoding four of the most distinctive:

**FEELING CALM**
Here, the perfect baby has softly cupped her hand, indicating that all is right in her world.

**FEELING TRAPPED**
Baby is restless. Note the way her index finger has symbolically "pinned" her thumb

**FEELING INSURGENT**
Baby is becoming volatile. An upraised fist always bespeaks a powerful sense of rebellion.

**FEELING OUTRAGED**
"What the hell do you mean: 'paper covers stone'?! Hold on, *nooooooo!* Don't swaddle me!"

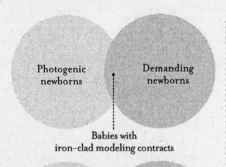

Babies with
iron-clad modeling contracts

Respected
breast-milk critics

## Premier Blends

**When struggling to grasp
the rareness of miracles, it helps
to view them as tiny subsets
of larger infant populations,
as diagrammed here.**

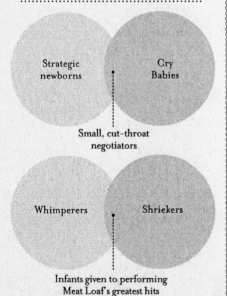

Small, cut-throat
negotiators

Infants given to performing
Meat Loaf's greatest hits

## The Telltale Poop

**To gauge your new baby's health,
well-being, innermost thoughts,
and ultimate destiny, monitor
her feces color. While a variety of
shades are considered normal in these
first weeks, others can indicate
cause for alarm.**

| | Color | Meaning |
|---|---|---|
| | Greenish black | Normal for first bowel movement |
| | Mustard yellow | Normal for breast-fed babies |
| | Ancestral gold | Normal for aristocratic babies |
| | Khaki | Will work weekends at the Gap |
| | French blue | Frankly, was hoping for an imported crib |
| | Slate blue | Will become involved with the CIA |
| | Egyptian green | Is the reincarnation of a pharaoh's dog |
| | Silver | Dangerously Warholian |
| | Peasant brown | Future kindly shoemaker |
| | Puke green | Will fight for his right to party |
| | Thistle | Itchy |
| | Dove gray | Normal for distant relations of the Brontës |
| | Sepia brown | Is living in the past |
| | Swamp green | Is slowly developing gills |
| | Jade green | Wouldn't mind having a dynasty |
| | Beige | Is a fuddy-duddy |
| | Cool gray | Prefers fewer hugs, thanks |
| | Burnt orange | Wants Grandma out of the house *now!* |
| | Mink brown | Has been eating fur |

# Miracle Bonding

### THE RISKS OF FAILING TO BOND WITH A NEWBORN ARE TOO UPSETTING TO CONTEMPLATE AT LENGTH. LUCKILY, WE ONLY HAVE TWO PAGES.

Also known as "attachment parenting," bonding is the process of gaining Baby's trust by responding promptly to her needs and creating a physical connection. It begins in the delivery room the instant her head starts to crown and indicates its desire for a comforting pat and a deep-conditioning hair mask.

As soon as Baby comes home, you and your partner will want to take turns strapping her to your chests like a large brooch to create a literal attachment. (See "Bound for Glory," page 36.) From this lofty vantage point, she'll see the world through your eyes as you enjoy your daily routine: cooking, gardening, flipping real estate, eating, avoiding sex, and, finally, JetSkiing. The constant proximity reassures her you'll always be there, and ultimately gives her the confidence to accuse you of smothering her when she's three or four.

*fig. 1*

Though the baby-care industry has devised countless tools designed to speed the attachment process—including "familiarity dolls" with which the parent is instructed to sleep, thereby imbuing the doll with his or her scent—don't overlook the standard C-clamp.

## Usage Note

In advanced parenting circles, the term "bonding" is the fourth most commonly used word, after "perfect," "caterwauling," and "num-num-num-num-num." Though primarily employed as a noun or an adjective ("Nice bonding weather we're having!"), it also functions well in adverb form ("The baby bit me bondingly") and as an imperative ("Quick, Allison, bond before Gustav loses any more self-worth!").

## Potential Dangers

The diagram at right ranks infants' needs from least to most crucial. Since bonding is the most critical of all, it follows that ignoring your miracle for even a few minutes can easily warp his entire life. As research conducted by drunken Australians has shown, incompletely attached perfect children tend to:

1. **Become socially withdrawn:** Instead of asking for a large, festive birthday party with forty guests, they may request a smaller gathering with only one or two circus elephants.
2. **Lack self-reliance:** Even as adults, they may insist that their parents accompany them everywhere, which is especially awkward if they choose to become astronauts.
3. **Adapt poorly to new situations:** They may grow fretful when the time comes to make the leap from congressperson to Speaker of the House and pee on their constituents.

### THE PERFECT BABY'S HIERACHY OF NEEDS

**Miracles require both sleep and aquatic prowess, but a strong attachment is bottom-line.**

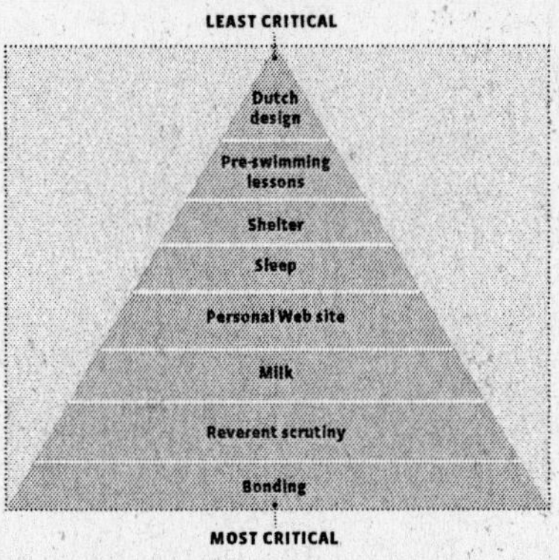

LEAST CRITICAL

Dutch design
Pre-swimming lessons
Shelter
Sleep
Personal Web site
Milk
Reverent scrutiny
Bonding

MOST CRITICAL

## Preventive Measures

Whenever Baby is just lying there contented, pointedly not needing you, attachment experts suggest you concoct a scenario that will require you to squeeze in more hands-on interaction. Some of their recommendations:

- **Hallucinate** a stray eyelash on Baby's cheek. Now you must gently brush it away.
- **Consider** the possibility that your infant lacks networking skills. Now you must introduce him to the basics of a proper golf swing.
- **Imagine** that angry Nazis have overheard you proclaiming your fondness for whiskers on kittens and crisp apple strudel. Now you must carry your baby across the Alps to safety, singing lustily.

# Survival of the Cutest

ZOOLOGISTS INSIST THESE NEWBORN
CREATURES RIVAL YOUR BABY FOR MIRACULOUSNESS.
IS THERE ANY CAUSE FOR ALARM?

## Baby Giraffe

**Evidence of superiority:** A rare sense of graciousness. Since its mother gives birth standing up, this gangly newborn plummets six feet to land on its skull, only to be drenched with a gush of afterbirth. Instead of fussing, the courteous giraffe calf simply hops up and frolics.
**Then again:** Your newborn is not inconvenienced by a nine-inch black tongue.
**Advantage:** Perfect Baby.

## Baby Bottlenose Dolphin

**Evidence of superiority:** Expert swimming skills. The newborn bottlenose leaves the womb in full motion and—following its mother's example—swims for an entire month without any sleep, happily suckling on sacs near its mom's anus.
**Then again:** Miracles rarely nuzzle anuses (or agree to be trained as military assassins).
**Advantage:** Perfect Baby.

## Baby Tiger

**Evidence of superiority:** Impressive survival instincts. Blind, inept, and boring, the newborn tiger cub is initially nothing to write home about. But in terms of self-directed snacking, it blows human infants away, making its first kill at only 18 months.
**Then again:** Your child knows better than to eat undercooked meat or poultry.
**Advantage:** Perfect Baby.

## Baby Spider

**Evidence of superiority:** Unparalleled creative flair. Few perfect babies can stand on their heads and spin pure silk out of their rear ends, no matter how many "Mommy and Me" craft classes they attend.
**Then again:** Your offspring, with only two knees, as opposed to the spider's forty-eight, is a relative joy to dress.
**Advantage:** Perfect Baby.

## Baby Pelican

**Evidence of superiority:** Bold expression. The starving chick throws itself at its parents' feet, writhing theatrically and even going into convulsions until it's fed.
**Then again:** A miracle may be moody, but she never indulges in cheap melodrama.
**Advantage:** Perfect Baby.

## Baby Horse

**Evidence of superiority:** Where to start? Not only can a new foal bash its own way out of an amniotic sac and see in two directions at once, it can also snort, squeal, nicker, neigh, blow, and trigger unconscious eroticomania in thirteen-year-old girls.
**Then again:** Horses can't vomit, not even when they've accidentally eaten cotton balls.
**Advantage:** Perfect Baby.

## Baby Kangaroo

**Evidence of superiority:** Extraordinarily early mobility. The "joey" learns to crawl as a fetus, wriggling from its mom's vagina to her pouch. Once there, it latches onto a teat with little to no help from a lactation expert.
**Then again:** The name "Joey" has zero cachet.
**Advantage:** Perfect Baby.

## Baby Sea Turtle

**Evidence of superiority:** Abandoned by its mother in an egg she buried on a beach, the hatchling must burrow to the surface and dash to the ocean on wee, clumsy legs before a feral pig can gobble it up. Then it calmly rears itself to adulthood entirely on its own.
**Then again:** Um, well . . .
**Advantage:** Stupid Sea Thing.

# Troubleshooting the Newborn

## DO NOT PANIC IF SOMETHING GOES AMISS—MOST MIRACLE MALFUNCTIONS ARE EASILY REMEDIED

### I.
### Baby starts hanging out with a bad crowd.

**Correct response:** Become "bad" yourself. Wear heavy eyeliner. Address Baby using 1920s street lingo: "Hey, Mac, I know I should mind my own potatoes, but these flim-flammers you're chinning with give me the heebie-jeebies." Once Baby grasps how dangerously cool you are, he'll reject the unsuitable playmates soon enough.

### 2.
### Newborn begins using voodoo masks as an intimidation technique.

**Correct response:** Firmly remove the mask. Do not show any fear and refuse to concede your authority, unless newborn starts to whimper. In that case, however, immediately fall under a voodoo spell that compels you to make funny barnyard-animal sounds twenty-four hours a day with an emphasis on quacks and moos.

### 3.
### Newborn ogles another woman's breasts.

**Correct response:** Consider yourself blessed. A born connoisseur, your baby is evaluating other milk sources, just as he will soon be choosing Chardonnays and Merlots. Politely ask the woman in question to hold still until he has satisfied his curiosity, then thank her warmly for her time.

Even perfect babies can manifest slight flaws, as you'll soon discover. Some pee too expressively. Others develop a steely gaze or seem determined to burn down your home. Fortunately, sensitive parenting can transform these rebels into model citizens whose arson ambitions are strictly limited to rickety old shacks. Outlined below are six of the most common miracle troubleshooting issues and how to deal with them.

### 4.
### Perfect newborn won't stop bawling.

**Correct response:** Babies communicate by crying. If yours persists in wailing after her basic needs are met, she obviously has important things to say. Hire a court reporter to transcribe each shriek phonetically. Once Baby realizes her howls are being immortalized, she'll screech far more comfortably.

### 5.
### Baby secretly gets Botox injections—can no longer express emotions.

**Correct response:** Get to the root of Baby's need to fight the aging process. Is she afraid she'll be overshadowed by more youthful-looking babies when it's time to compete for coveted nursery-school places? If so, reassure her that the same tightening effect can be achieved with a powerful hair band.

### 6.
### Newborn suddenly turns into a manatee.

**Correct response:** First and foremost, do not criticize your bloated child/creature. While it's certainly true that you didn't sign up to raise a manatee and may have trouble finding Bottega Veneta booties that fit his massive fins, view this as a rare opportunity to live underwater at enormous expense.

# The War of the Poses

## SECRETS TO IMMORTALIZING YOUR MIRACLE ON FILM

As photographic subjects go, the newborn's commitment to holding a pose is not always ideal. However, if you have an engaging concept, patience, and forty-six memory cards, it *is* possible to inflame her innate passion for the art. *The Perfect Baby Handbook* asked professional fashion lensers for their advice:

1.
Begin your next photo session, the pros suggest, by respectfully asking Baby to leap in the air gripping a bunch of balloons.

2.
If Baby yawns, indicating that she finds this idea clichéd, buy some time. Lay her on a solid-colored blanket and shoot an extensive series of blinking and drooling studies.

3.
Interrupt shooting if Baby gets fussy or beckons for a misting of Evian water. Use this time to double-check your child's face for traces of food, flaky skin, smudges, or unmistakable signs of fury.

4.
Abruptly break for lunch/breast-feeding.

5.
After chins have been wiped and tempers have cooled, the experts suggest you urge Baby to strike an ungainly pose and hold her head at a glamorously awkward angle.

6.
If your newborn averts her eyes, scrap that idea and brainstorm some fresher concepts. What if, for example, Baby crouches in the street surrounded by abandoned cars that are engulfed by flames? Or leads a group of third-world children in a march to freedom? Or, alternatively, engages in a hair-pulling "fight" with another model?

7.
As you wait for feedback, shoot a few candids of Baby staring at you blankly.

# 3.

## Basic (Yet Perfect)
# BABY CARE

When cultivating greatness, the first step is to establish a schedule. Perfect babies have much they want to achieve each day and like to know that regular blocks of time have been set aside for key activities such as feeding, sleeping, smiling, the gleeful destruction of Mommy's new *Vanity Fair*, and slack-jawed staring.

Facilitating Baby's agenda is exhausting, but you'll benefit, as well. As author Kazuo Ishiguro observes in *The Remains of the Day*, there is honor in serving a demanding master. Of course, in his novel, the master is an immoral British aristocrat and the servant a blindly obedient butler, and neither is under two years old, but the principle still vaguely applies.

If your infant shows no interest in a routine, don't worry. A miracle who moves from activity to activity in a completely haphazard manner can still grow up to be a successful air-traffic controller or even a social butterfly. That said, a schedule is preferred and some are more miraculous than others.

The legendary routine outlined over the next two pages had its public debut in the home of Mohinder and Alison Singh of Phoenix, Arizona in 2008. Though the Singhs' timetable is ideal for infants from four to six months old, it can inspire us all.

# Timing is Everything

A prototypical routine for a perfect baby,
age four to six months

**7:00 a.m.** . . . . . . Baby wakes up.

**7:01 a.m.** . . . . . . Surveys her domain.

**7:03 a.m.** . . . . . . Notes that Exersaucer is dusty again.

**7:04 a.m.** . . . . . . Announces this news piercingly.

**7:07 a.m.** . . . . . . Enjoys day's first feeding; forgets Exersaucer crisis.

**7:31 a.m.** . . . . . . Burps triumphantly.

**7:32 a.m.** . . . . . . Savors brisk lavender aromatherapy massage.

**7:40 a.m.** . . . . . . Endures diaper change by flipping through *Bon Appétit.*

**7:45 a.m.** . . . . . . Considers toy options.

**7:48 a.m.** . . . . . . Compresses Squeezy Snake while murmuring what sound like conjugations of the French verb *péter* (to fart).

**7:50 a.m.** . . . . . . Is interrupted by Daddy, who's off to work.

**7:51 a.m.** . . . . . . Cocks head at nautical motif on Dad's tie. Sailboats? *Really?* In mid-winter?

**7:52 a.m.** . . . . . . Waves goodbye to Dad in adorably "feeble" manner. Throws in crying fit for free.

**7:59 a.m.** . . . . . . Pulls self together.

**8:00 a.m.** . . . . . . Indulges Mom's new fascination with the Turtle Tooter Shape Sorter.

**8:08 a.m.** . . . . . . Finds thoughts drifting to Martin Scorcese's early work.

**8:14 a.m.** . . . . . . Falls in and out of love with a keychain.

**8:20 a.m.** . . . . . . Baby Pilates (10 minutes).

**8:30 a.m.** . . . . . . Poking Things (20 minutes).

**8:50 a.m.** . . . . . . Poking Things that Turn Out to Be Mom's Eyes.

**8:51 a.m.** . . . . . . Rolls over.

**9:01 a.m.** . . . . . . Performs loose interpretation of the Bride's solo dance from Martha Graham's 1944 ballet *Appalachian Spring.*

**9:10 a.m.** . . . . . . Silent Meditation (1 minute).

**9:11 a.m.** . . . . . . Semi-Silent Meditation.

**9:15 a.m.** . . . . . . Meditative Shrieking.

**9:30 a.m.** . . . . . . Second feeding.

**10:00 a.m.** . . . . . Nap.

**12:30 p.m.** . . . . . Wakes up; coughs discreetly.

**12:33 p.m.** . . . . . Diaper change.

**12:38 p.m.** . . . . . Declares that new diaper makes her look chunky.

**12:40 p.m.** . . . . . Supervises alterations.

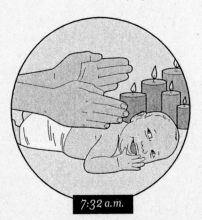

7:32 a.m.

9:01 a.m.

**12:45 p.m.** . . . . . .Third feeding.

**1:20 p.m.** . . . . . . .Visits with dignitaries, heads of state, or (on slow days) Mom's friend Rachel.

**1:45 p.m.** . . . . . . .Perfects vacant facial expressions (10 minutes).

**1:55 p.m.** . . . . . . .Sobs (15 minutes).

**2:10 p.m.** . . . . . . .Power nap.

**2:12 p.m.** . . . . . . .Reviews atomic structure of favorite amino acid.

**2:27 p.m.** . . . . . . .Lollygags (3 minutes).

**2:30 p.m.** . . . . . . .Meets with perfume experts re: development of signature scent.

**3:00 p.m.** . . . . . Fourth feeding.

**3:30 p.m.** . . . . . . .Nap.

**5:20 p.m.** . . . . . . .Wakes up abruptly.

**5:22 p.m.** . . . . . .For disorienting moment, thinks she's trapped in the jungle in 'Nam

**5:23 p.m.** . . . . . . .Oh the *filth*, the baking sun, the *stinking* Vietcong with their *foul*—

**5:25 p.m.** . . . . . . .Diaper change.

**5:30 p.m.** . . . . . . .Fifth feeding.

**6:00 p.m.** . . . . . . .Grasps concepts.

**6:10 p.m.** . . . . . . .Does other things to concepts.

**6:14 p.m.** . . . . . . .Decides not to be a lesbian. For now.

**6:15 p.m.** . . . . . . .Romps! (8 minutes).

**6:23 p.m.** . . . . . . .Prepares for Daddy's return by adjusting face into mournful expression.

**6:25 p.m.** . . . . . . .Greets Daddy resentfully.

**6:26 p.m.** . . . . . . .Fails to resist pleasure of being tickled by Daddy.

**6:30 p.m.** . . . . . . .Reclaims her dignity.

**6:32 p.m.** . . . . . . .Completes clapping class homework.

**6:46 p.m.** . . . . . . .Drastic Mood Swings (14 minutes).

**7:00 p.m.** . . . . . . .Sinks into soothing bubble bath.

**7:01 p.m.** . . . . . .Recalls with dismay the need to actually be washed.

**7:03 p.m.** . . . . . .Diversionary Splashing.

**7:30 p.m.** . . . . . .Final diaper change.

**7:36 p.m.** . . . . . .Watches Daddy's lips move as he reads something educational aloud.

**7:46 p.m.** . . . . . .Interrupts to request Accuweather forecast.

**7:50 p.m.** . . . . . .Final feeding.

**8:12 p.m.** . . . . . .Burps national anthem.

**8:15 p.m.** . . . . . .Says good night to the stickers on nursery window.

**8:16 p.m.** . . . . . .Waves at parents.

**8:20 p.m.** . . . . . .Effortlessly drifts to sleep.

**8:37 p.m.** . . . . . .Tormented by dreams of dusty Exersaucer.

**8:40 p.m.** . . . . . .Wakes up screaming.

**8:43 p.m.** . . . . . .Though still trembling, manages to execute a few soothing shadow puppets.

**8:47 p.m.** . . . . . .Drifts to sleep, this time for good; dreams of complex quilting patterns.

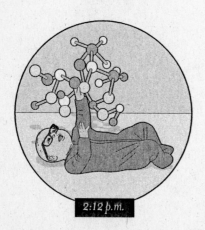

2:12 p.m.

8:43 p.m.

# Bound for Glory

## UNDERTAKING THE BABYWEARING CHALLENGE

**I**f you could make a minor difference in your baby's future just by eating ninety-three sheets of sandpaper, would you? Of course you would, unless the sandpaper contained trans-fats or wasn't completely fresh.

Yet a surprising number of couples hesitate when it comes to babywearing—the traditional art of binding one's baby to one's body. Perhaps they don't realize that infants who are laboriously lashed to their caretakers with seventeen-foot-long Balinese cloths are more likely to overachieve and wear Hollywood-style turbans later in life.

Oddly, even parents who are open to the babywearing challenge sometimes think they lack the dexterity to tie one on. How absurd. Anybody who can execute a simple two-sided, overhand hitch-knot in torrential winds is more than nimble enough. A step-by-step guide to some popular variations:

*fig. 1*

**Stomach-to-Stomach Wrap**

1. Lie on your back with Baby balanced on your tummy.
2. Clench your seventeen-foot Balinese binding cloth in your teeth.
3. Carefully levitate your body until both you and Baby are hovering several inches above the floor.
4. Tie and go.

## Advanced Twins Wrap

1. Using a thirty-four-foot Balinese cloth and two experienced assistants, bind the twins to any body part they choose.
2. Cantilever a stimulating educational mobile off your left shoulder.
3. Knot securely.

## "Expert Included" Wrap

1. Using a sixty-eight-foot Balinese cloth and a small construction crane, lash on your infant, his car seat, and Dr. William Sears, noted babywearing authority.
2. Balance a log on head for a note of third-world authenticity.
3. Dash off to Baby's play date.

# Competitive Breast-feeding

### SEVEN WAYS TO NOURISH
### WITH DISTINCTION

According to conventional wisdom, a woman must nurse her infant to be a superior mother. What nonsense, insisted a leading medical group in a recent public statement: "We, the American League of Pediatrics, would like to clarify. It is not necessary to breast-feed to be a superior mother; it's necessary to breast-feed spectacularly. By way of further clarification, let us add, "Go, moms, go! Be aggressive! Be aggressive! *B-e-a-g-g-r-e-s-s-i-v-e!*"

Given such calls to action, it's no wonder certain women nurse as though they're trying to one-up each other. Even if you opt out of this lively dynamic, you may want to familiarize yourself with the key areas of competition:

1. **Most spiritual experience:** Moms who excel here call up busy friends while nursing to announce that they've reached nirvana—only to become so overwhelmed by the "breast-feeding high" that they "can't quite talk . . . just now. Sorry." For bonus points, they comfort others who are not so blessed: "It's not your fault, Katherine.

Your hormones must be underachieving. Have you had your oxytocin levels checked?"

2. **Most arduous ordeal:** This title goes to the competitor who can most vividly describe surreal pain. For instance, Contestant A might say, "For me, breast-feeding is like having my nipples slammed repeatedly in a dresser drawer," only to be

trumped by Contestant B: "How awful. For me, it's more like being attacked by a very sweet and gifted king cobra."

3. **Most versatile:** In this category, outstanding contestants must demonstrate the ability to breast-feed in unlikely situations—for instance, crouching in a less-than-spotless Guatemalan bathroom or onstage at the Metropolitan Opera.

4. **Most efficient:** This title typically goes to the sort of woman who nurses while writing elaborate e-mails about identity politics, tracks her miracle's feedings with a digital wristband, and still finds time to pump while flying her invisible plane.

5. **Longest endurance record:** Claiming this honor is a simple matter of nursing until Baby is at least four while evincing an awesome attitude: "If I can make it all

the way into Andrew's fifth year, I'm going to reward myself with a lacy bra!" Bonus points for "tandem nursing" a toddler and newborn simultaneously.

6. **Strictest elimination dieter:** To shine here, moms must banish the highest number of potentially baby-irritating foods from their diets, until they're eating nothing but brown rice and poached chicken (". . . and yet Baby is *still* cranky . . ."), and are ready to murder their husbands for one-fifth of a Tuscan Three Cheese Kettle Chip.

7. **Most uninhibited:** This is perhaps the easiest way to win. All the triumphant mother has to do is brave public nudity in breast-feeding sweaters that are so off-the-shoulder they are more properly described as on-the-ground.

# INTRODUCING SOLID FOOD

*You'll meet less resistance if you serve it—artfully—on the breast.*

**Some experts proclaim that pears, and only pears, will do when Baby's ready to move past milk. Yet just as important as what foods you choose is how you present them. Try these irresistibly arrayed haute-cuisine menus:**

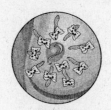

**SPRING BACCHANAL**
Dust breast with pulverized graham crackers, then drizzle on pomegranate puree. Dot with mashed banana rosettes using a parchment piping bag (tip #17). Finish with mint.

**SAVORY ADVENTURE**
Wield piping bag (tip #31) to extrude mashed avocado in radiating lines. Array with sun-dried-tomato pasta, then garnish with a curl of local artisanal cheddar. Serve alfresco.

**GARDEN OF DELIGHTS**
Weave strips of fresh papaya and jicama into a "garden trellis." Attach edible flowers. Dab on sugar-free jelly to simulate dewdrops. Convince a butterfly to hover nearby.

# Safety Begins...Everywhere

## HOW TO BABY-PROOF ALL POTENTIAL
## DANGERS ON EARTH

You could pay consultants a fortune to block power outlets, lock cupboard doors, and move everything breakable to Guam, but why bother? Thanks to foolproof plastic products designed to neutralize threats both in and outside the home, it's just as easy to safeguard Baby yourself. A comprehensive guide:

I.

## Natural Hazards

Protecting your miracle from all known organic risks may sound exhausting, but it's not. You barely have to worry about fog, so that's a relief. And a single, all-purpose fern barrier can subdue even the most menacing ferns. For everything else (animal, vegetable, or mineral), it's a simple matter of buying the appropriate plastic devices. Here, we render a prickly beast impotent.

### Baby-proofing a wild porcupine

1. Approach the porcupine warily, humming Abba's "Fernando."
2. Explain that Baby wants to interact with it both safely and productively.
3. Swiftly attach a half-inch polyurethane quill guard to each of its 350 needles.
4. Repeat step 2 as often as required.

2.

## Manmade Threats

Manufacturers of dangerous objects like pickaxes and tiered wedding cakes rarely take baby safety into account. While loving parents once had to tell their infants sternly, "Sorry, Baby, this unstable, multi-level dessert is out of bounds," now they can just order customized safety guards online. Here, we quickly infant-proof a notoriously pointy Parisian icon.

### Disabling the Eiffel Tower

1. Special-order vast plastic corner-bumpers from monument-safety.com.
2. Bribe *les gendarmes* to clear the area of tourists and outraged locals.
3. Lower bumpers into place via helicopter, taking care not to crush any stubborn street performers.
4. Admire tower from a safe distance.

# Know the facts: Thirty-seven percent of perfect babies will be accosted by the Italian paparazzi before the age of two.

## 3.
## Paranormal Dangers

Traditional safety guards are less effective when it comes to dealing with supernatural aggressors such as zombies, werewolves, shape-shifting aliens, goblins, wraiths, banshees, mummies, and gremlins. In these unusually irritating cases, it's more strategic to encase Baby himself in life-preserving polystyrene. Here, we confound an impish unseen spirit.

### Neutralizing a poltergeist attack

1. Enclose Baby in body armor from a reputable antipoltergeist outfitter.
2. Stand guard, humming "Kung-Fu Fighting."
3. Fend off objects the ghost hurls at Baby until a Braun PowerMax blender catches you unawares.
4. Remain unconscious while Baby quiets the intruder with his disarming charm.

## ADDITIONAL SECURITY RISKS

Certain threats are too wily, too fidgety, or too abstract to baby-proof and must simply be avoided. Never expose Baby to the following:

- Q-Tips
- Orlon®
- Churlish kittens
- Sarcasm
- Unsuitable relatives
- Caricaturists
- Ming the Merciless
- Falling rocks
- Immobile rocks
- The Playboy mansion
- Dingy white geese
- Accordians
- Unflattering sunlight
- Dazzling special effects
- *Sturm*
- *Drang*
- Unsolicited mail
- A humdrum existence
- Surprisingly powerful mints
- Gruel
- The so-called "Queen" of Narnia
- Frowny faces
- Joyce Carol Oates
- Chasms
- Press-On Nails
- Sharp spoons
- Amateur theatrics
- Mysteries involving old clocks, twisted candles, or dancing puppets
- Unfolded napkins
- Minotaurs
- Topiary animals near old hotels
- Secret herbs and spices
- Dangerously inviting tubas
- Cats in hats
- Flimsy igloos
- Company loving types of misery
- Lukewarm-air balloons
- Tarts
- Restless glaciers
- Head-sized thimbles
- Dashikis
- Black Forest (German territory)
- Black Forest (cake)
- Untested recipes
- Combination skin
- Finger bowls
- Billie Holiday's less upbeat songs
- Unsupervised pom-poms

# Advanced Slumber Strategies

CONVINCE YOUR LITTLE ONE TO SLEEP
THROUGH THE NIGHT—BEFORE ALL THE OTHER
BABIES ON THE BLOCK

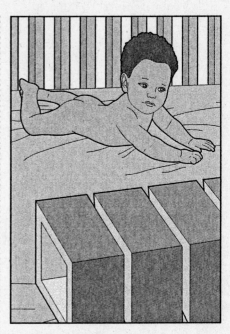

I.

## Adopt a three-toed sloth

Often babies who have failed to master uninterrupted unconsciousness simply need a role model. Most Dutch pediatricians recommend this sloth, a congenial animal that sleeps up to eighteen hours a day and has a knack for making wakefulness seem uncool. Notice how this miracle is so eager to please his new sloth, he can barely keep his eyes open, let alone scream for nourishing breast milk.

**Safety tip:** Do not adopt a *two-toed* sloth. Plagued by a sense of inadequacy, the breed attacks anyone with a larger array of toes.

2.

## Bore Baby with dull art

This popular Lithuanian technique involves surrounding your infant with unstimulating masterpieces. For example, Baby need only stare at Donald Judd's unrewarding minimalist sculptures (see illustration) for two minutes before pleading for the oblivion of sleep. As an alternative, have your sister tell Baby about her dream, the one where she tries on seven hundred pairs of slingback shoes.

**Safety tip:** When lifting dreary neoclassical paintings more than fifteen feet wide, remember to use your legs, not your back.

S ome miracles find the concept of snoozing through the night passé. After dark, they prefer to pursue less sensible hobbies such as weeping inexplicably or playing mah-jongg. What's a frustrated parent to do? Friends and neighbors try to help by supportively bragging about their own babies' sleep prowess: "It's like Maximilian enters this nine-hour coma! We find it quite uncanny!" Don't be fooled: Likely as not, these smug parents are sneakily using one of these cutting-edge European techniques.

 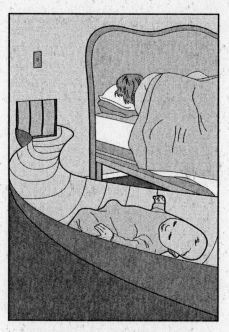

### 3.
### Churn butter doggedly

Re-creating the familiar whooshing sound of the womb can lull even skeptical babies to sleep. While some parents fuss with noise machines and others brandish blow dryers, they're wasting their time. As the Swedes have discovered, no sound triggers infant slumber more effectively than that produced by the simple, picturesque act of throttling a wooden butter churn for four to seven hours every night.

**Safety tip:** It's not advisable to eat the twenty-nine pounds of butter you'll be producing each week in the form of garlic toast.

### 4.
### Invest in a baby conveyor belt

Another Swedish innovation, this device ferries the miracle between your bed and her nursery, rocking her gently as she travels. While giving Baby a degree of independence, it zips her past you frequently enough that she can sense your soothing presence. And there are few moments more tender than when Baby shoots through the plastic infant door like a case of imported beer.

**Safety tip:** Though engineered to the highest standards, the conveyor belt is not suitable for babies over twenty-five years of age.

# Lingering Concerns

### MASTERING OTHER CHALLENGES—
### FROM SELECTING LULLABIES TO ACCLIMATING
### YOURSELF TO THE SCENT OF POO

**Which songs are the most calming at bedtime?** The traditional "Hush, Little Baby" works well, as does "Have You Never Been Mellow" by Olivia Newton-John.

**What if my miracle prefers to remain unmellow?** Keep singing—unless he files a formal complaint or angrily bats an object.

**He's angrily batting an object right this minute. What should I do?** It depends. How's his accuracy?

**Pretty amazing. He rarely misses.** In that case, hire a top sports lawyer to soothe him with the promise of a $23 million professional baseball contract.

**How can I make bath time more mentally enriching?** Turn it into a series of learning moments. As you wash your miracle's shoulder, use the Mandarin word for "shoulder": "Now we wash your little TK. Scrub your little TK, scrub, scrub, scrub!" Then move onto other body parts: "Now we scrub your little TK. . ." and so on.

**What if Baby protests that Mandarin is too easy?** Give him a brisk shower instead.

**How can we tell whether our miracle has justifiable objections to our parenting or is just being fussy?** It's never easy. Depending on the situation, you and your partner may need to commission an opinion poll of a thousand randomly selected Americans.

**Really? What if our judgmental childless friends are all randomly selected?** Do you mean Sarah, Pete, Lars, Naomi, Jared, Akiko, Portia, R.J., and Melissa?

**Yes. Especially Akiko.** You will have to trust in the polling process—and pay Akiko off.

**Can poor diapering damage my infant psychologically?** Yes, particularly if your face betrays disgust for Baby's feces. Familiarize yourself with the odor: Burn feces-scented candles or spritz on an appropriate fragrance. Chanel No. 2 is a great choice for moms, while most dads find Turd for Men Body Splash quite bracing.

**What if my boss protests? Our office has a no-scent policy.** Explain to your boss that, although you respect his thoughtful dictates, it's crucial for you to smell like poo.

# 4.

## Miracle-Worthy
# GEAR

**D**isturbing historical fact: A shocking number of the world's most promising babies, individuals who might have gone on to accomplish truly great things, were raised without sufficient gear.

Consider the gifted kid born in Malaga, Spain, on October 25, 1881. This ill-fated baby did not even have a basic bouncy seat, let alone an ergonomic highchair with an adjustable footrest. What his humble parents lacked in equipment, they tried to make up for with names, exhaustively christening him Pablo Diego José Francisco de Paula Juan Nepomuceno María de los Remedios Cipriano de la Santísima Trinidad Martyr Patricio Clito Ruiz y Picasso— a name so cumbersome he usually went by his initials, P.D.J.F.D.P. J.N. M.D.L.R.C.D.L.S.T.M.P.C.R.Y.P. Or sometimes just "Picasso."

Although this child eventually scraped out a living as a painter, it's hard not to imagine what he *might* have achieved had he enjoyed the benefits of a jogging stroller with a multi-position canopy and a good-sized underseat basket. When you factor in his natural drive, it's no stretch to say that he could have become a legendary stockbroker with a nice vacation home in Aspen.

And that's just one example. With an effective car seat, Eli Whitney would surely have invented something less frivolous than the cotton gin. Similarly equipped, Captain Kangaroo might have been an admiral, or Dr. Seuss a well-regarded urologist. The list goes on.

It's not always a given, of course, that gear would have made the difference. Take Virginia Woolf, pioneer of the stream-of-consciousness novel. Even if her parents had ponied up the cash for an automatic baby-wipes warmer, would

**Since it's hard to predict which product will unlock Baby's genius, acquire as much gear as your home can elegantly accommodate without exploding.**

anyone remember the author of *To the Lighthouse* and *Mrs. Dalloway* today except as someone with a funny nose and a love for the run-on sentence?

More often, though, the sense of a lost opportunity is clear and haunting. Does anybody doubt that the poet Sylvia Plath, at one point a promising accountant, could have grown up to create some truly exciting tax write-offs if her parents had purchased a digital ear thermometer (had one been available in 1930s Massachusetts)?

Does anybody question that a sleek, Scandinavian bassinet at just the right moment might have given Neil

Armstrong the wherewithal to tackle a major planet like Saturn, instead of a minor moon?

Or that Pyotr Ilich Tchaikovsky—who loved notes and was clearly destined to be a stenographer—would have left behind a legacy of eerily accurate interoffice memos instead of a few measly symphonies if only he'd had access to a Fisher-Price Rainforest Jumperoo?

In short, although there's no guarantee that gear will catalyze your miracle's genius, this is one area where you can't afford to stint. You're probably wondering, "But how much gear is too much gear? And which award-winning innovations should I purchase first?" Here's a good rule of thumb: Since it's impossible to predict just what products will do the trick, acquire as much gear as your home can elegantly accommodate without exploding.

Carefully weigh the potential benefits of each item. Even a seemingly uninspiring carriage like the Alieta V2 Stroller in mocha by Vito Verago with a five-point harness, all-wheel suspension, and an adjustable water bottle holder (for larger bottles) can shape your baby's destiny. Had Napoleon Bonaparte enjoyed something similar as an infant, who knows? Instead of dying in disgrace on the lonely island of St. Helena, he might have whiled away his years in relative glamour as a Manhattan panhandler.

According to local legend, his parents, Tracy and Paul Bonaparte, never forgave themselves.

# Raising the Bar

Navigating the complexities of the baby
product world can be daunting.
Take this test to see how much you already know.

**1. The pacifier was invented by a pacifist: true or false?**
a. True.
b. False.
c. I don't feel particularly challenged by this quiz so far. Could we get serious? I have a conference call.

**2. In terms of stroller physics, what does m stand for in the following equation: F = d(mv)/dt?**
a. Miles.
b. Momentum.
c. Mass, but why are you invoking Newton's Second Law? No stroller is designed with acceleration in mind.

**3. Complete this phrase: Nunchaks are:**
a. Traditional African teething aids.
b. Breast-feeding support pillows.
c. Could I just point out that the baby over there on the right is using his nunchaks without the supervision of a qualified martial arts instructor?

**4. Why do so many infant product names include the word lil'?**
a. Because babies are traditionally little.
b. Because babies are traditionally lil'.
c. This question seems peripheral, but if you insist: The word lil' helps fetishize infants as precious creatures who must be pampered and extravagantly dressed—thus fueling the consumerism cycle. It's crass marketing like this,

I should add, that leads to exploitative children's beauty pageants.

**5. How many products does it take to doom Baby to a tragic childhood on the beauty pageant circuit?**
a. Lots.
b. An infinite amount.
c. Okay, I get it. My interest in testing my knowledge is just a joke to you people, isn't it?

**6. Can a high-quality baby monitor detect the sound of angels?**
a. No.
b. Maybe ... if they're chatty angels.
c. [bitter silence]

ANSWER KEY: If you answered mostly Cs, you are a know-it-all and should have no trouble navigating the complex world of baby gear.

# Wheels Within Wheels
## THE COMPLEXITIES OF CHOOSING STROLLERS

Given the plethora of options, carriage shopping is bound to bewilder. As you debate each model's pros and cons, niggling questions arise, such as "Does Baby really need a stroller that can handle the terrain of uninhabitable planets?" or "Just what makes a question niggle?" In their confusion, some parents buy too many buggies. The truth is: You can meet all of Baby's needs with just these ten.

### 1. The Lightweight Stroller
Built for speed and agility. Completely collapsible. Light as a clunky feather.
**Ideal when:** Baby wants to zip out of the house before she and Mommy go completely mad.

### 2. The Deluxe Heavy-Duty Stroller
Sturdy European design. Mows down insufficiently nimble pedestrians. Clears old-growth forests. Both shock-and bank-account-absorbent.
**Ideal when:** Baby wants to impress other parents who only bought the Standard Heavy-Duty model.

### 3. The Travel-System Stroller
Removable car seat lets you transfer a sleeping infant from stroller to Volvo; also attaches to ski lifts, gondolas, and Guatemalan donkeys.
**Ideal when:** Your miracle is passed out but nonetheless filled with wanderlust.

### 4. The Cargo Stroller
Originally developed by the Pentagon. Features twenty-nine storage pockets and seven decorative pockets.
**Ideal when:** Baby feels uneasy leaving home without his entire collection of Toy Trucks Designed for Compulsive Clutching.

### 5. The Unfocused Meanderer
Developed in close collaboration with new-age singer Enya and her many cats.
**Ideal when:** Your infant wants to blow off her schedule and wander through a California poppy field until 2:07 p.m.

### 6. The All-Weather Jogging Stroller
Can handle any conditions, thanks to a rain canopy, a built-in snowplow, sleet shields, and a tornado deflector.
**Ideal when:** Baby is yearning to deliver the mail in rural Minnesota.

### 7. The Thoroughly Pimped-Out El Camino Stroller
"Lowrider" design with white sidewall tires, garish decals, and crushed velour upholstery. Inspired by thuggish infants in the San Fernando Valley.
**Ideal when:** Your little one urgently needs to regain his street cred.

### 8. The Eco-Stroller
Crafted from live, sustainable bamboo that must be watered daily and hacked back with a machete when it gets too unruly.
**Ideal when:** Baby wants to surprise Al Gore with an impromptu visit.

### 9. The Classic Victorian Carriage
Evokes that genteel era when infants were sedated with opium and forced to lie on their backs in traditional prams.
**Ideal when:** Your miracle would like to remind you loudly that he's not a drugged-out Victorian who's willing to forgo a view.

### 10. The No-Frills Stroller
Homemade of straw, mud, and wood. Uncomfortable, but builds character.
**Ideal when:** Baby is feeling overindulged and wants a reality check. Also available: The Okay-Maybe-a-Couple-of-Frills-but-That's-It-Sweetie Stroller.

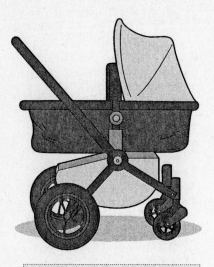

1.

**FORMIDABLE**
THE HEAVY-DUTY STROLLER

4.

**SENSIBLE**
THE CARGO STROLLER

7.

**RACY**
THE EL-CAMINO STROLLER

10.

**SOBERING**
THE NO-FRILLS STROLLER

# Double Agents

### DISPENSE WITH CHORES *AND* IMPRESS YOUR BABY AT THE SAME TIME WITH THESE DAZZLING "TWO-IN-ONE" INVENTIONS

### The Soothe 'n' Seal™ Combination pacifier and tape-dispenser

Some say it's impossible to calm a shrieking miracle and gift-wrap professionally at the same time. They're right. It's easy, however, to achieve sloppy, semi-professional results once you stun Baby into silence with this tape-dispensing nipple.

**Tip:** To further wow your offspring, rip the tape off with your teeth.

### Stinky Maid™ Combination potty and self-directing vacuum

Though miracles toilet-train early, they soon tire of pooping so predictably. This irresistible potty reengages Baby in the defecation process, zooming her robotically across carpets as it sucks up dust and debris.

**Tip:** If Baby expresses a desire to suck up financial records instead, start her on low-yield treasury bonds.

### Thoughtful Coast Guard Mummy™ Combination breast pump and fog horn

Imagine how your baby's respect for you will grow when she witnesses you pumping milk while sounding a deep, haunting warning that might help a ship avert disaster.

**Tip:** Before using this device for the first time, arrange to live in a vast blanket of fog off the coast of Nova Scotia.

### Disaster Björn™ Combination baby carrier and jet pack

Should an unforeseen threat—say, a strange man with a hacking, phlegmy cough—necessitate a quick escape while Daddy and Baby are on the town, this discreet device will rapidly blast both to safety.

**Tip:** Do not overaccelerate or you may end up in orbit, causing Mommy to worry.

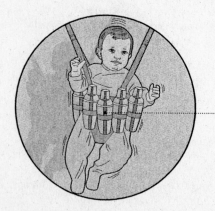

### Bar-Hop Baby™ Combination infant bouncer and cocktail shaker

Miracles love to help. Next time you entertain, give yours a pivotal role. Fill this device's five shakers with martini fixings, set Baby to bouncing, and within seconds, you'll have everything you need to grow increasingly irresponsible.

**Tip:** To respect Baby's nap schedule, have your guests drop by shortly after breakfast.

# Ideally Equipped

Answers to eternal questions about purchasing gear—including who,
what, where, when, why, and "Pardon me, *how* much?"

**What's the biggest mistake parents make when buying baby paraphernalia?** Going about it in a willy-nilly fashion. If you spend too recklessly, it's easy to end up with a vast mountain of junk, instead of a vast mountain of quality merchandise.

**So, basically, it's about buying the right mountain?** Precisely.

**Do I really need a bassinet?** Yes. However, a simple woven Moses basket works well, too, especially if you need to hide Baby among the bulrushes in the River Nile to save him from a power-mad pharaoh.

**I'm so envious of parents who invent bestselling baby products. I have a few spare minutes next Thursday—should I use that window to invent and patent one of my own?** Absolutely! Unless that time would be better spent promoting the germ-eliminating night-light your spouse patented last week.

**Is it true that Hammacher Schlemmer makes a decent playpen?** Hammacher Schlemmer would never use the offensive term "playpen."

**Why is it offensive?** It evokes pigs with a poor work ethic. The company does, however, sell a $2098 Gently Hindering Privacy Zone that's guaranteed to divert Baby for hours so you can gossip on the phone.

**What makes you think I gossip?** It could be that scandalous story you constantly repeat about your neighbor Cynthia—the one who bought her infant an acetylene torch for "educational reasons"?

**Oh god, her. Did you hear the latest about her husband?** Vain fellow? Got his stomach liposuctioned? Drives a hybrid?

**Yeah, him. Anyway, get this. He's telling people that their baby is being recruited by Princeton. Something about an all-day IQ test ... it's such complete baloney. Ridiculous. Everyone knows Princeton hasn't launched its infant-recruitment program yet.** Your neighbor obviously meant Yale.

**Yale?! Shut up! Is that a gear-related question?**

**No, but hold on—** Did you have any additional gear-specific queries today? Because otherwise—

**Who cares about gear?!** Your neighbor Cynthia and her taut-tummied husband had plenty of thoughtful questions the other day. They seemed truly committed.

{Lengthy pregnant pause} Um, okay, okay ... I suppose we could discuss a few highchair nuances. But I only have an hour. That's cutting it tight.

# Rating the Teething Toys

MIRACLES WITH TENDER GUMS LOVE CHEWING
HARD, SMOOTH ITEMS, BUT BEWARE: NOT
EVERY TEETHING PRODUCT WORKS EQUALLY WELL.

## Your Friend Pat's Cell Phone

**Strengths:** Engages Baby with amusing beeps and ringing sounds.
**Weaknesses:** Tends to be rudely grabbed by Pat during so-called emergencies; traumatizes Baby by "dying" when exposed to even moderate amounts of slobber.
**Bottom line:** Would be more effective if Pat were less possessive.
**Rating:** 3 (out of 10)

## Your Father-in-Law's Platinum Credit Card

**Strengths:** Can be dented with satisfying ease—causing blabby in-laws to lapse into a lovely, furious silence.
**Weaknesses:** Has an inadequate thousand-nibble limit.
**Bottom line:** Not bad, until Baby and your father-in-law start fighting over who's going to pay for dinner.
**Rating:** 5.5

## Your Cousin Valerie's Designer Sunglasses

**Strengths:** Are quite prestigious and valuable, as Valerie keeps reminding you so fretfully; lend teething process a note of glamour.
**Weaknesses:** As it turns out, can be "totally &@$%-ing ruined" rather easily, requiring a visit to small claims court.
**Bottom line:** Baby's favorite!
**Rating:** 10

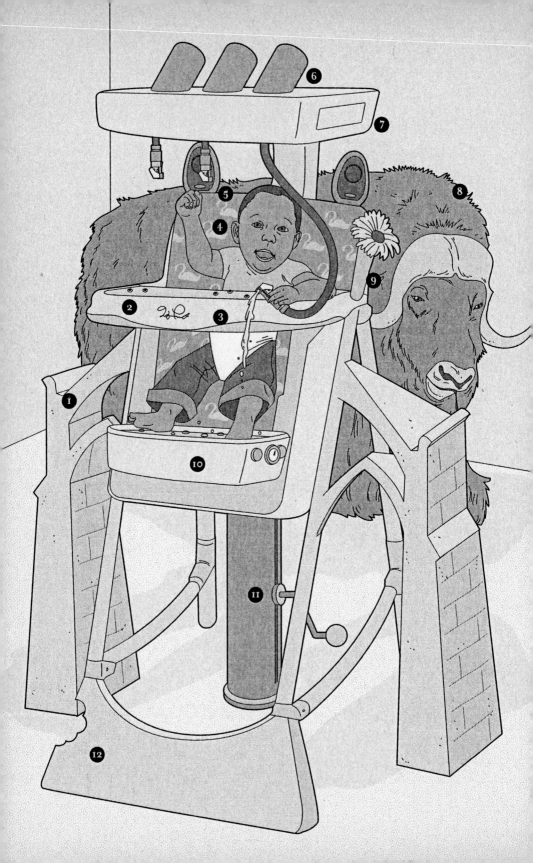

# The High Life

## PRESENTING THE ULTIMATE IN ELEVATED
## SLOPPY-EATING SEATING

It's easy to find a safe highchair. Or an affordable highchair. Or even a sophisticated model conceived by a renowned lingerie designer. But try finding a highchair that satisfies all the top concerns of today's discriminating parents. Not easy. Here's a sneak preview of the many advantages of the X90Q56, a prototype that comes quite close.

1. **Stable:** Reinforced with granite flying buttresses inspired by Gothic architecture.

2. **Adaptable:** Includes four interchangeable tray options—basic, subdivided, Butler's, and embalming.

3. **Distinguished:** Has been personally autographed by noted chef Mario Batali.

4. **Comfortable:** Upholstery is stuffed with swan's down from descendants of the original Ugly Duckling.

5. **Educational:** Discreet micro-speakers expose Baby to cuisine-related vocabulary phrases such as béchamel sauce, Bibb lettuce, and "Sorry, I'm a vegan."

6. **Expressive:** Overhead sauce dispensers equip the miracle to squirt a selection of colorful fruit purees relatively near his food.

7. **Safe:** Equipped with side air bags (not employed here) in the unlikely event the chair tips over in gale-force winds.

8. **Portable:** Includes an ox that will willingly haul the 750-pound chair into other rooms.

9. **Decorous:** Incorporates a sleek, stainless steel bud vase.

10. **Detoxing:** A footbath scented with therapeutic juniper and pointless patchouli soothes Baby's aching arches.

11. **Versatile:** Can be effortlessly height-adjusted up to seventeen feet tall in case Baby's nanny is a giantess.

12. **Digestible:** Is 38 percent edible in the event of sudden food shortages.

---

## THE EARLY REVIEWS

### What parents had to say about the X90Q56 in preliminary tests:

"At first, we weren't sure the ox would be adequately nurturing. But now he's part of the family! Our cats love to tease him."
—*Bonita and Andy Dyson*

Great chair! The bud vase is a nice touch. I wasn't happy, however, when bats took up residence in the flying buttresses."—*Elise K. Blouin*

"The airbags came in handy one night when gale-force winds swept through our kitchen and our giantess nanny, who normally deals with such matters, was out at a movie."
—*Poppy Tigle and Albert Ngo*

"The X90Q56's edibility was a life-saver. As my sister's wedding party can attest, it's delicious served on a Triscuit." —*Tara Leguizamo*

"I'd have liked it even more in gun-metal gray."—*J. Hitchcock*

"Just knowing that the down in the cushions comes from a long line of once-unattractive swans fills me with a sense of security."
—*Deion Morrison, Jr.*

# Quantity Control

## FORECASTING BABY'S GEAR STORAGE NEEDS
## (IN CUBIC FEET) OVER THE NEXT TWO DECADES

As the years pass, a miracle's gear collection grows exponentially. Take art supplies: While a gifted newborn can squeak by with a box of crayons and a kiln, she'll soon need a proper fresco-painting set, including a trough of wet plaster and a small Portuguese-style chapel.

This raises a practical question: How exactly do you store a chapel? Some parents build a backyard gear barn. Others rent a cheap warehouse just off the

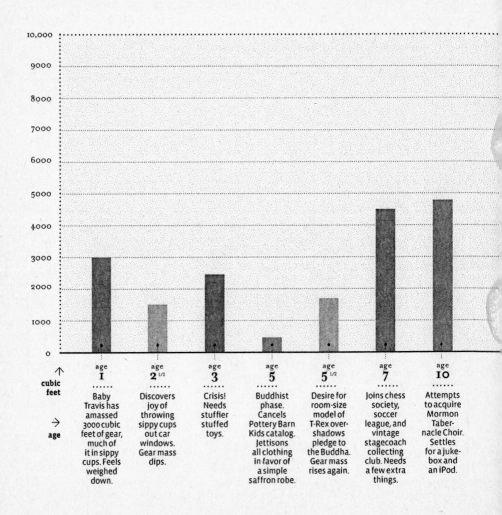

| | age **1** | age **2**½ | age **3** | age **5** | age **5**½ | age **7** | age **10** |
|---|---|---|---|---|---|---|---|
| cubic feet → age | Baby Travis has amassed 3000 cubic feet of gear, much of it in sippy cups. Feels weighed down. | Discovers joy of throwing sippy cups out car windows. Gear mass dips. | Crisis! Needs stuffier stuffed toys. | Buddhist phase. Cancels Pottery Barn Kids catalog. Jettisons all clothing in favor of a simple saffron robe. | Desire for room-size model of T-Rex over-shadows pledge to the Buddha. Gear mass rises again. | Joins chess society, soccer league, and vintage stagecoach collecting club. Needs a few extra things. | Attempts to acquire Mormon Tabernacle Choir. Settles for a jukebox and an iPod. |

interstate. For convenience's sake, Sam and Lyla Robinson went underground, constructing an eight-level basement beneath their modest San Diego bungalow. When their son urgently needs any of his 2,300 possessions, he just descends by freight elevator into the basement's eerie depths and optically scans the object's location code. Within fifteen minutes, either Sam or Lyla delivers the desired equipment to his playroom. It's a near perfect system.

Of course, the size of your offspring's arsenal can suddenly drop. As this bar graph tracking the gear-mass fluctuations of Houston-based miracle Travis Lemmley shows, these dips usually coincide with the child's realization that he's not living the simple life. You'll want to anticipate such declines when planning your own long-range storage plan.

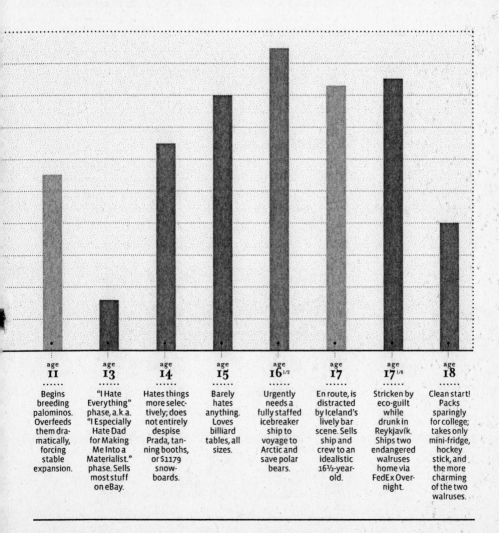

age **11**
Begins breeding palominos. Overfeeds them dramatically, forcing stable expansion.

age **13**
"I Hate Everything" phase, a.k.a. "I Especially Hate Dad for Making Me Into a Materialist." phase. Sells most stuff on eBay.

age **14**
Hates things more selectively; does not entirely despise Prada, tanning booths, or $1179 snowboards.

age **15**
Barely hates anything. Loves billiard tables, all sizes.

age **16**¹/²
Urgently needs a fully staffed icebreaker ship to voyage to Arctic and save polar bears.

age **17**
En route, is distracted by Iceland's lively bar scene. Sells ship and crew to an idealistic 16½-year-old.

age **17**¹/⁸
Stricken by eco-guilt while drunk in Reykjavík. Ships two endangered walruses home via FedEx Overnight.

age **18**
Clean start! Packs sparingly for college; takes only mini-fridge, hockey stick, and the more charming of the two walruses.

# Essential Impulse Buys

It may seem risky to shop the internet at 4 a.m. when you're sleep-deprived
and have no judgment. Still, many parents find the wee hours
a convenient time to fill these gaping holes in their gear collection.

**1. Solid Gold Pacifier**
Equally practical in either
10- or 18-carat ore.
*not-actually-that-soothing.co.uk*

**2. Family-Sized Rocking
Horse** Seats up to seven
humans of various sizes.
*oppressive-togetherness.com*

**3. Leprechaun Taser**
Efficiently immobilizes
gold-pacifier thieves.
*hands-off-my-baby.com*

**4. Matching High Chair,
High Sofa, and High
Ottoman** Not suitable for
low ceiling'd rooms.
*toddler-of-distinction.net*

**5. Lil' Arc de Triomphe**
Baby-proofs your home the

Nineteenth Century way.
*historically-significant-infant-safety-
gates.com*

**6. Little-to-No Wind
Chimes** A brilliant solution
for those overly calm days
and nights.
*nursery-emergencies.com*

**7. Infant Pedometer**
Counts up to fifteen
arguably vigorous steps.
*break-a-tiny-sweat.com*

**8. "Cindy the Centipede"
Cake Pan Set** Includes
145 non-stick, aluminum
(mostly leg-shaped) pieces.
*OverachievingMom.net*

**9. Chatty Yam** Another
fine product from the

makers of the popular
Murmuring Tofu.
*ingratiating-food-shaped-toys.com*

**10. The Original Anti-
Bacterial Planet Cover**
Protects Baby from
unsanitary continents.
One size fits all Earths.
*SterileFun.com*

**11. Newborn Hair
Scrunchie** Holds four to
twelve wispy follicles securely
(available in pink or pinker).
*TinyCoiffure.com*

**12. Baby's First Laugh Track**
Features a supportive mix of
chuckles, hoots, and guffaws.
Completely snicker-free.
*oh-my-god-baby-is-hilarious.com*

*fig. 1*

What parent can
resist this sturdy
child-safety
gate inspired
by the Arc de
Triomphe?

# 5.

## Perfecting Baby's
# SELF-ESTEEM

The demands of constantly overachieving can weigh heavy on tiny shoulders. As Anthony Gus Greenberg-Wong, age 13 months, of Los Angeles, explains in notably precocious full sentences: "It's like, whenever it's time for me to throw food at my parents' faces, they start looming over me, all eager to be precisely strewn with mush. But you know what? Sometimes my arm gets sore and all I want to do is lie around with an ice pack and ponder alienation themes in the *X-Men* films. I feel so inadequate."

Daisy Chloe Reynolds, an extremely early walker in Fair Haven, New Jersey, says she faces pressure from a more surprising source: "Now and then I need to fart, right? But even if I squeeze one out impeccably, there's always some Gund stuffed animal with a taffeta bow giving me that deadpan, beady-eyed expression that says, 'Was that really necessary?' It's hard to stay upbeat."

Another frequent complaint among perfect babies is the unrealistic expectations that their parents and nannies place upon them to be high-maintenance. Admits Freddie Crane, a Glendale, Arizona-based perfect baby: "They act so disappointed if I'm not demanding attention or throwing pointless tantrums. I mean, tyranny is fun and everything, but occasionally you just want to be tender and meek. Like that Gerber baby."

Adds Greenberg-Wong: "Meekness? Yeah, good luck with that. Utterly taboo. Wimp out for two seconds and suddenly you've got 'self-esteem issues,' and they're frantically Googling and validating your feelings and trying to sleep in your bed. And you know what? I think that's poopy!"

Judging from this regression to baby talk ("poopy"), a classic indication of damaged self-worth, Greenberg-Wong is in real peril. And, although it appears his parents are responding appropriately with focused Googling and "co-sleeping," it may be a case of too little, too late.

Do not let this happen to you. While it's important to challenge Baby with high expectations, never pressure her to perform. When a miracle is allowed to progress at her own astonishing rate in a healthy, supportive atmosphere, she'll feel no need to rebel. (As a precaution, however, you may want to claw off the eyes of particularly judgmental stuffed animals and pre-splatter your face with mush to relieve stress at meal times.)

Although this laid-back approach should help instill Baby with superior self-esteem, never assume she's out of danger. After all, few miracles are as eloquent as Greenberg-Wong; at times, the feedback you receive will be as ambiguous as a wet burp. That's why it's best for you and your partner to take turns monitoring Baby day and night for the seven red flags vividly depicted at right.

## PERFECT MISERY

Identifying poor self-esteem takes a practiced eye. Sometimes even a miracle's own parents can miss these warning signs

1. **Becomes withdrawn:** Baby may try to "hide" in a corner of his crib or—if he is athletically gifted—in the limbs of a mighty White oak.
2. **Loses interest in playing:** Even with

his favorite high-powered compound binocular microscope.

3. **Neglects appearance:** Loses fascination with Velcro closures. Wears hair in greasy ponytail à la Rambo. Ignores posture tips.

4. **Writes bad poetry:** Worrisome themes include bleakness, doomed ladies from Nantucket, and Clifford the Big Incompetent Dog.

5. **Avoids eye contact:** At times, you may feel like you're only getting half of your child's attention.

6. **Dwells on the past:** Obsessively watches a video of his own birth, mouthing the words "Push, Mommy! Push!"

7. **Develops an uncharacteristic fixation with material possessions:** Hints heavily that a snakeskin-covered rattle might improve his mood. Briefly, it does.

# Crawling Tall

IF YOUR MIRACLE DOES FALL INTO A SELF-ESTEEM
SLUMP, THESE TECHNIQUES SHOULD
QUICKLY GET HIM BACK ON HIS HANDS AND FEET AGAIN

**Provide unconditional love**: Unless Baby specifies a few conditions of his own—in which case, modify your love for him accordingly.

**Use positive reinforcement:** Praise your perfect infant often, being as precise as possible. Instead of saying, "Yay! You stood up on your own," try this variant: "Yay! You stood up without resorting to the various winches and miniature cranes we provided for your use."

**Establish rules:** Limits help babies feel more secure. Start with simple, enforceable concepts such as,

"No more than three cookies per day." Then gradually up the ante, forbidding your miracle to pull the the dog's tail or challenge your rules at the Supreme Court level.

**Permit mistakes to happen:** Allow your perfect baby to solve problems on her own. Mask any sense of irrelevancy you might develop so she won't feel compelled to pause and nurture you.

**Screen Baby's friends:** Negative influences can ruin the self-esteem rebuilding process. Reject prospective playmates who appear too aggressive, too gloomy, too destined to win an Olympic medal, or too middle-aged.

**Support healthy risks:** If there's no scope for failure in your miracle's life, he'll never truly appreciate success. Just make sure you're there for him, ready to wipe his tears, whenever he attempts to make an overly ambitious shrimp risotto.

**Schedule togetherness moments:** Encourage Baby to carve out a little quality time for you each day. Then just have fun! Pop popcorn (before discarding it for nutritional reasons). Play patty-cake, avoiding actual physical contact in case she internalizes it as abuse. Act out your favorite scenes from *Grease*. Pass out beside her crib in exhaustion.

**Create a positive environment:** Never call your partner names like "liar" or "slob" in Baby's earshot. Substitute more upbeat phrases like "ingeniously evasive woman" or "triumphantly unmotivated man."

**Help Baby understand his emotions:** Try statements like, "I can see that you're feeling upset and conflicted today, perhaps with an undercurrent of angst. Oh, sorry. I stand corrected: 'an undercurrent of impatience for me to stop talking.'"

**Avoid comparisons:** Never tell your miracle that she is "smarter than Confucius" or "cuter than the goddess Aphrodite." Perfect babies are sticklers for accuracy and may demand an independent government inquiry.

## LEARNING TO SHINE
*The benefits of manual labor*

**You can boost Baby's self-confidence significantly by allowing her to help out around the house. Some simple chores most miracles enjoy:**

- Autographing the fresh laundry.
- Unmaking the bed so it looks less "uptight."
- Washing the biscotti.
- Refrigerating the car keys.
- Watering the iPods.
- Resizing the dishes (smaller, more jagged pieces preferred).
- Dusting Daddy's eyebrows.
- Deodorizing the Brie.
- Distributing the cutlery more evenly throughout the house.
- Polishing her figure skating trophies.

Best Skater

# Beyond Co-sleeping

## TO REAP THE FULL BENEFITS OF TOGETHERNESS, PARENTS MUST DO MORE THAN SNORE

## 1.
## Co-pooping

**Technique:** As soon as Baby starts making pre-poopy faces, alert your spouse so he or she can drop everything and drive home from work. That way, assuming traffic is on your side, the entire family can go stinky together.

**Self-esteem benefits:** By associating bowel movements with joy and acceptance, you will remove any stress surrounding them and give your child the confidence she'll need to poo alone some day, possibly during her senior prom.

## 2.
## Co-unicycling

**Technique:** Introduce your infant to the balance challenges of riding a unicycle, then do your best to keep up.

**Self-esteem benefits:** Your little one will feel at least seven inches taller, depending on how you adjust his seat's height. On the down side, Baby may grow too dependent on the belief that you'll always be there tenderly embarrassing him. Such infants, the experts insist, do not even attempt to pedal one-footed, backward, up a hill alone until it's much too late.

Devotees of attachment parenting try to maintain constant physical contact with their infants, insisting this gives the child both a stronger sense of security and enough time to deep-cleanse mommy's pores. While some of these selfless caretakers go so far as to share a bed with their offspring—a practice known as "co-sleeping" or "slowly forgetting what sex is"—the truly ambitious go even further, incorporating these advanced strategies.

## 3.
## Co-composing

**Technique:** Play to each other's strengths. If Baby has a way with barely comprehensible words, you supply the jaunty, hook-laden tune. Tap into your shared experiences to identify universal themes such as love, loss, and the eternally spinning wheels on the bus.

**Self-esteem benefits:** By churning out top-forty hits, Baby will slowly develop a sense of a fan base. You'll know she's gaining confidence when she starts tossing out your first rough melodies, insisting you are capable of greater work.

## 4.
## Co-being Adorable

**Technique:** Occasionally, Baby may feel too unsure of strangers to delight them thoroughly on her own. Support her efforts with co-giggling, co-blinking, co-face-scrunching, and the co-delivery of "three accountants walk into a bar" jokes.

**Self-esteem benefits:** Not only will your child grow up secure in the knowledge that she's hilarious and has an unusually scrunchy face, she will never be tempted to enter a bar filled with drunken CPAs.

# Cautionary Tales

## THE SAD STORIES OF THREE INSENSITIVELY PARENTED MIRACLES

**M**ost perfect babies bounce back from a self-esteem crisis in no time. One minute, they're shrieking inconsolably; the next, they're as happy as clams—which is to say, as happy as clams en route to a shrink's office for weeks of cathartic, play-based therapy can be. Unfortunately, not all perfect babies recover so breezily. Consider these sobering case studies:

### Julie P. Smithers (b. 1970)

**Demonstrated perfection at:** Age nine months by painting a detailed mural of the food chain on her nursery wall.

**Self-esteem collapsed when:** Her mother failed to praise Julie's drawing of an elk, citing "hoof inaccuracies."

**Tragic consequences:** Today, although Julie earns seven figures as a Manhattan litigator, laughs often, and shares a historic penthouse with her hunk of an Egyptologist husband, she still shivers briefly whenever she's surrounded by elk.

### Ben Quincy Morris (b. 1983)

**Demonstrated perfection at:** Six months by snipping his dad's hair into an asymmetrical, new-wave "Flock of Seagulls" style, adding volume and shimmer with a fast-freeze spray.

**Self-esteem collapsed when:** His father, a funeral director, thoughtlessly shampooed away the results just nine weeks later.

**Tragic consequences:** As an adult, Ben runs a visionary Web-development company, knits superbly, and constructs his own lighthouses. He was recently named Seattle's Sexiest Billionaire but, for reasons we can only guess at, his hair lacks both bounce and shine.

**One false move, one lukewarm hug, one indelicately worded endearment—and your perfect baby can grow up to be a perfect basketcase.**

**Melissa Sue Ngo** (b. 1976)

**Demonstrated perfection at:** Twenty-two weeks by declaring war on kitschy pop-culture memorabilia, stripping her parents' home of countless Snoopy figurines.

**Self-esteem collapsed when:** The Ngos neglected to remove some Strawberry Shortcake wallpaper at which she'd pointedly frowned, invalidating her taste.

**Tragic consequences:** Today, Melissa is the Secretary of Defense and Time's Person of the Year. Her compulsive need to wear Beverly Hills 90210 buttons in bed, however, speaks of unresolved issues.

---

## SAFETY ADVISORIES

Do not attempt to cultivate self-esteem until you have read the following guidelines.

1. When fostering self-respect near a medium- or large-size wood chipper, always wear protective eye gear.

2. Remember to look both ways before encouraging independence in twins.

3. Never promote Baby's self-worth if you're feeling the slightest bit tired, groggy, bleary, woozy, run down, tuckered out, exhausted, bushed, enervated, pooped, outta gas, or obsessed with your thesaurus.

4. Never instill confidence until Baby has signed and dated the instillation order.

5. No running indoors, even if you and Baby are rapidly approaching a self-esteem breakthrough.

6. When knighting Baby, use a dull blade and ask a reigning sovereign to supervise.

7. Stay focused. Otherwise you may accidentally cultivate one of these other psychological conditions:
  · *Elf-esteem:* A problematic susceptibility to imps.
  · *Delft-esteem:* A reverence for blue-and-white china.
  · *Shelf-esteem:* A tendency to hold storage systems dear.

# Unconditional Doves

## SECRET CODES, TRAINED BIRDS, AND OTHER EMERGENCY PRAISE TECHNIQUES

While praise can nourish a miracle's confidence, babies who inspire too many routine compliments from friends and family will soon grow numb to positive feedback. If you notice your child's eyes glazing over, reengage him at your earliest convenience with these more sophisticated strategies:

**Enlist the help of feathered friends:** Painstakingly train white doves to alight on Baby's outstretched arms every time he successfully outstretches them. Keep a moist cloth handy.

**Try transmitting praise in code:** Choose simple, discreet phrases only you and Baby understand. "Stalag, Stalag, the fever is rising!" might mean, for instance, that Baby has correctly gripped her sippy cup.

**Bury a positively reinforcing treat in the middle of the hedge maze at Hampton Court:** Few parenting experiences are more rewarding than watching your miracle eagerly navigate this seventeenth-century labyrinth to find his prize. *Warning:* Baby may give in to a childish urge to prune.

**Forge a telepathic connection:** Think laudatory thoughts; wait until Baby psychically receives them. Be patient.

**Send praise via telegram, Norman Rockwell-style:** Arrange for a fresh-scrubbed messenger boy to deliver an old-fashioned "wire" to your home on bicycle. Convince your neighbors to rush out of their houses at the sound of his merrily clanging bell dressed in gingham aprons or overalls, waving their hands with excitement.

**Engineer a miracle:** Persuade a body of water to part as Baby triumphantly crawls through it. Though the Red Sea is a traditional choice, Lake Huron has also been known to cooperate. *Warning:* Your miracle may be allergic to seaweed. Ask your doctor.

# A Word About Discipline

According to the theory behind the new "gentle discipline" approach, naughty miracles don't want to hear hollow threats. They prefer to hear mealymouthed remarks that strenuously avoid any hint of negativity.

Gentle disciplinarians never shriek "Stop screaming or else!" at their toddlers. They murmur: "Now, Thaddeus, perhaps you recall that we rarely endorse screaming in our home." Although countless parents have found this method an effective way to bewilder children, an advanced version called "extra-gentle discipline" is delivering even better results. Which is right for you?

| conflict | gentle discipline | extra-gentle discipline |
| --- | --- | --- |
| Baby repeatedly bangs toy against a big-screen television. | "$4,000 TVs are not for hitting, Joshua" | "$4,000 TVs are not for hitting, Joshua. Let me give you a $750 model you can demolish instead." |
| Baby turns face away when parent offers food. | "Will it work for you, Sybil, if we try this again in five or ten minutes?" | "Will it work for you, Sybil, if I dance around your chair performing a high kick until I realize that nothing will make you yield?" |
| Baby throws tantrum in Toys "R" Us; refuses to leave. | "I know you're upset right now, Stewart, but would it be okay if we talk about this in the car?" | "In know you're upset, Stewart, but would it be okay if I evacuated the building and sealed the doors so you can regain peace of mind at your own glacial rate?" |
| Baby gropes a fragile vase, even though parent forbade her to do so. | "Can you tell me why you did that, Amelie? Maybe next time, we can come up with ideas together that will help us avoid such misunderstandings." | "Can you tell me why you did that, Amelie? Maybe next time I can be a different person, perhaps a wizened Russian diplomat, who mysteriously commands your respect." |
| Openly defiant, Baby continues to grope the frail, priceless vase in question. | "I'm glad you realize, Amelie, that you are the one who decides what you do. But I would ask for some cooperation when I suggest another approach." | "I'm glad you realize, Amelie, that I'm a doormat you can walk all over. But I would ask you to walk on my forehead where the imprint of your tiny feet will be most visible." |

# A Parent's Guide to Surveillance

## LEARN TO SPOT THESE NINE SELF-ESTEEM DESTROYERS BEFORE IT'S TOO LATE

No miracle wants to spend months developing her self-worth only to have some callous stranger diminish it slightly. Yet this happens all the time— even, as one San Francisco couple discovered, in midair. Adam and Marcia Hancock, en route to Rome with their baby Sophia, were horrified when their elderly seatmate declined to smile at Sophia, citing his need to prepare for an impending crash landing.

As parents, it's your duty to shield Baby from such thoughtless and damaging influences. Start by learning to steer clear of the nine common offenders depicted in this typical, seemingly harmless urban scene.

*fig. 1*

1.
**The Antique-Store Owner Who Bans Strollers:** Sure, he wants to protect his fragile merchandise. But what about the pain Baby feels when denied the right to comparison-shop for secretary desks?

2.
**The Geisha:** Makes Baby feel indiscreet and overbearing, not to mention poorly cinched.

3.
**The Shusher:** Tries to limit the miracle's freedom of expression; is stubbornly unimpressed by Baby's three-octave crying range.

4.
**The Secret Language of Birthdays:** This unnecessarily rude astrology book (on fortune teller's table) claims that miracles born on October 4th are incorrigible, headstrong, and foolhardy, while July 22nd babies ("The Day of Occupational Fluctuations") are unlucky and stressed out.

5.
**The Territorial Parent in the Park:** Refuses to let her child share his toys with Baby, claiming that they have just been permanently sterilized at great expense. "In Switzerland."

6.
**Any Road in a Yellow Wood that Fails to Diverge:** Prevents Baby from taking the road less traveled, ultimately forcing him to stay overnight in a Cleveland hotel.

7.
**The Snotty Hipster:** Contemptuously dismisses your offspring as a "yuppie accessory"; refuses to believe that Baby has already shown considerable interest in Brooklyn-based novelists.

8.
**The Catatonic Animal:** Just lies there, declining to play with Baby, bringing little to the table beyond an indifferently twitched tail.

9.
**The Pretty Girl Whose Biological Clock Has Yet to Begin Ticking:** Is too busy being sexy and carefree to covet your miracle, which leaves him feeling ignored and somewhat confused.

# Uplifting Messages

## ENCOURAGE POSITIVE FEELINGS WITH THESE SUBTLY UPDATED NURSERY RHYMES

### Rosy Prospects

Ring around the rosie,
A pocket full of posies,
Ashes, Ashes,
We all open thriving
cupcake bakeries!

. . . . . . . . .

### Masterful Boat Management

Row, row, row your boat
Purposefully down the stream
Ecstatically, ecstatically,
ecstatically, ecstatically
Life is but one triumph
after another.

. . . . . . . . .

### Wednesday's Genius

Monday's child is fair of face,
Tuesday's child is full of grace,
Wednesday's child is so
expertly medicated,
You barely notice the whole
"full of woe" thing.
And, of course, he's quite
the little workaholic.

. . . . . . . . .

### I'm a Perfectly Proportioned Teapot

I'm a perfectly
proportioned teapot.
Let's leave it at
that, shall we?

### The Pease Porridge Tasting Menu

Pease porridge hot!
Pease porridge chilled!
Pease porridge in the pot,
Nine days old . . .
a very desirable vintage.

. . . . . . . . .

### Bonjour, Sun!

Rain, rain, go away—
No, you've been perfect!
You're incredibly fun.
It's just that we're looking for
something . . . less moist

. . . . . . . . .

### Itsy-Bitsy World Leader

The itsy-bitsy spider
Was obviously
malnourished . . .
Hardly a worthy role model.
Let's focus instead
on Dwight D. Eisenhower.

. . . . . . . . .

### Bravo, Humpty, Bravo!

Humpty Dumpty sat on a wall.
Humpty Dumpty nimbly
alighted from the wall.
As expected, he triumphed
at the Regional Wall-Sitting Finals,
Then took the gold at Nationals.
All the King's horses applauded wildly,
Even though it's almost physically
impossible for horses to clap.

# 6.

## Advanced
# MOBILITY

At first, a perfect newborn barely twitches. He lies in one place, exuding a Stonehenge-like grandeur. He sleeps, he eats, he radiates competence, and that's about it. It's all exceptionally predictable. However, as Baby becomes an infant on the move with places to go and Russian-language tutors to see, you can't always be sure what he'll do next.

Some miracles roll over obsessively. Others start nosing about used book stores. Especially precocious babies have been known to attempt the Locomotion, an early 1960s dance which involves jumping up, jumping back, acquiring the knack, and making a chugga-chugga motion,

leaving themselves wide open to charges of disorderly conduct.

Not all perfect babies develop so scandalously, of course. Most adhere more closely to the milestone schedule outlined on page TK. Try not to become too fixated on timetables or expert forecasts, though, or a neurotic panic may set in.

That's what happened to Russell and Theodora Rosen, who'd been given every reason to assume that their miracle Steven would be trampolining by twenty-one weeks. However, once Steven was positioned on his sixteen-foot octagonal trampoline ($1199, with safety enclosure cage), instead of bouncing seven feet into the air, he merely performed a quick sequence of hand-jive gestures and fell asleep.

The Rosens were rattled. They swore each other to secrecy in case news of Steven's sluggish development became widely known. The Internet offered no explanation. Doctors were mystified; one specialist had the nerve to suggest that the couple had misassembled the trampoline, using ordinary lug nuts instead of quality macadamia nuts, which angered the Rosens until they recalled that poor Dr. Hill suffered from dementia.

Meanwhile, Steven was quietly devising his own solution out on the trampoline. He tried frenzied hip movements. He tried crossing and re-crossing his legs with gusto. In the end, he simply hired a forklift operator to hoist him seven feet above the trampoline's surface. When the Rosens came home from emergency couples therapy to find their infant son perched precisely where they'd envisioned him, they learned a lesson all parents should heed: Miracles may not perform a skill "correctly" or on schedule, but they will usually concoct a brilliant creative workaround.

# All the Upright Moves
### A STEP-BY-STEP GUIDE TO THREE CLASSIC DEVELOPMENTAL BREAKTHROUGHS

## Basic Push-Up Sequence

1. **Achieves lift-off:** Once the miracle has exhausted the pleasures of scrutinizing your carpet at extremely close range, she will raise herself into a push-up position.

2. **Learns to "fly":** Supporting her weight on her tummy alone, Baby will start playing airplane—charging you $5 for an in-flight snack pack or $10 for a light fresh meal.

3. **Demands hidden wires:** Soon after, Baby will begin "soaring" across the tops of trees as "Nim-Nim" in her first Chinese action-adventure movie, *Drunken Master: The Reckoning.*

## Standard Sitting Sequence

1. **Sits supported:** At first, you'll need to prop Baby up with throw cushions, bolsters, or small boulders, whichever your miracle finds most effective.

2. **Sits unsupported:** As your child's muscle tone improves, he'll be able to take a seat with no assistance—in some cases, not even from a chair.

3. **Ensconces himself:** Eventually, he'll seek out a higher vantage point from which to monitor his Fisher-Price Little People for signs of insurrection.

## Typical Standing Sequence

1. **Stands with assistance:** Almost all perfect babies need a helping hand at first, but don't be presumptuous: Yours may prefer an ebony-wood cane.

2. **Masters balance:** Once your miracle learns to stay upright on her own, she will begin to assert her independence—rather fiercely at times.

3. **Segways:** If all goes well, Baby will soon be poised atop a miniature Segway Personal Transporter as the urban fabric of Paris whizzes by.

---

### A POINT TO PONDER

**"A baby of ordinary talent will always be ordinary, whether he travels or not; but a baby of superior talent (which I cannot deny myself to be without being impious) will go to pieces if he remains forever in the same place."**

*—Wolfgang Amadeus Mozart, Age 2, 1758*

# Literary Revolutions

It's no surprise that "rolling over"—one of the great developmental milestones—has been immortalized in literature again and again. Three moving passages to read aloud to Baby.

## A Rolling-Over in Regency England

*Excerpted from*
### THE WILSONS (1814)
*by* JANE AUSTEN

E ven as a babe in swaddling, Anne Wilson possessed a will that bedeviled her mother, a lady of severely limited genius and forty bonnets. "Whatever shall I do with her?" cried that lady. "When all the other newborn girls in Tarryton have rolled over days ago, my Anne *refuses* to fling even a single limb in the counterclockwise direction!"

"As you so routinely inform me, my dear," said Mr. Wilson, peering up from his tiny book, "and yet I fail to see the tragedy in a non-rotating infant."

"Why, our dear neighbors, sir! How grievously concerned they will be!"

"Ah," said he. "Still, if Anne is not inclined to whirl for their gratification, I am sure those gossips will be only too happy to revolve around her."

His daughter, it should be said, did not much care for the smallest Tarryton girls' way of rolling over, observing in their feeble revolutions yet another scheme to captivate future husbands. "I should sooner die a spinster at fourteen months," she often thought, "than attempt to curry favor with a gross motor skill."

In truth, however, Anne was far too spirited a child to live wholly unrotatingly. In the privacy of her chambers, she had been rolling crosswise, lengthwise, angle-wise and otherwise for a period of some weeks. It was there, just as she had completed a full one-and-a-half with a layback twist, that the infant Lord Cornwall scooted in unannounced, an interruption that filled young Anne with anguish, fury, and no small measure of secret delight.

## A Clean, Well-Lighted Roll

*Excerpted from*
### A MOVEABLE BASSINET
### (1925)
*by* ERNEST HEMINGWAY

It was five in the morning. The baby on the bed was not settled. It was a boy baby and, so, a restless baby. He would not settle until he had done the thing his father, a man with few pleasures beyond the pursuit of animal flesh, had done so boldly in his own babyhood.

The baby looked up. The ceiling looked down. It laughed at his weakness and impotence, though not out loud. It was a ceiling, after all, not a castrating woman.

"I will do it," the baby said. "I will roll from back to front." But he knew it was no good to try. Not then.

At dawn, sunlight filled the room. The baby rolled now and it was good. His lovely hip obeyed his will, his shoulder leapt from the bed like a bobtailed deer.

The thing was done. For a while, the shame passed. And then the baby went out for a plate of mussels and a Pernod.

## One Roll Is Not Enough

*Excerpted from*
### TWIRLINGS OF THE DOLLS
### (1971)
*by* JACQUELINE SUSANN

Jennifer had only been in the pulsing, tumultuous, cockamamie city a week when she rolled over for the first time. The New York press went "mad" and soon every two-bit producer in town was on the horn, flooding Jennifer's nursery with offers. An engagement to roll twice-nightly at La Mambo! A crawl-on part in the Broadway smash *Arrivederci, Sally!* Jennifer was so over-stimulated she didn't know whether to laugh or cry. Finally, she chose crying, having not yet mastered laughing.

"Come here, you beautiful, golden brat," said Jennifer's mother, a brassy broad who couldn't articulate the mixed-up emotions she felt for her meritorious kiddo. "Don't know where you got it, dollface," she spat. "Not from me!"

As the next months flew by in a daze of parties, bib fittings, and work, work, work, Jennifer saw other jazzily revolving babies give in to the temptations. Uppers, dexies, rollies, anything to make them sparkle: "Colic cures" they called them. "What a laugh!" thought Jennifer. She'd seen the toll these little boosts took. Missed cues. Imperfect rotations. Slow declines into Sapphic thrill-seeking.

"I need to get off this crazy merry go-round," she decided, "and onto a nice, Vermont swing set!" But the next day, a sparkling, unforgettable Tuesday in May, Hollywood came calling . . .

---

## FURTHER READING

BOTH THIS AND
THAT SIDE OF PARADISE
*by F. Scott Fitzgerald*

TO SIT ON A MOCKINGBIRD
*by Harper Lee*

LITTLE CRAWLING WOMEN
*by Louisa May Alcott*

THE STAND
*by Stephen King*

# Going Concerns
### ANXIOUS QUESTIONS
### ABOUT AMBULATORY DEVELOPMENT

**Our miracle is really quite stagnant. How can we encourage him to move?** Sit him down in front of a mirror. Once he realizes that his reflection is duplicating even his slightest gestures, he'll crawl off briskly—outraged that you brought a copycat baby into his home.

**What's the difference between wriggling and wiggling?** Wriggling propels Baby forward. Wiggling, on the other hand, is non-productive and vulgar. No one has ever made it to the top merely by wiggling except for the little piggy who went to market and stripper Gypsy Rose Lee.

**The brochure for my local baby-gym claims its play facilities will allow my miracle to enjoy "an extensive system of tunnels and ramps." Is that even safe?** It appears that this so-called "gym" is actually a twelve-lane freeway.

**Our baby hates "tummy time." Help!** Have you tried giving her a thirty-minute

---

## MOTION STUDIES

**Three easy exercises to help you identify with your miracle's motor challenges**

You can study your baby as exhaustively as you like, but until you walk a mile in his socks, you'll never really understand what it's like to make your way through society with doll-sized arms, bow-legged limbs, and a head that weighs as much (figuratively speaking) as a Jeep Grand Cherokee.

The following routine was developed in 2008 by the esteemed Cincinnati Institute of Precision Parenting in collaboration with Footwear Addicts Anonymous, the National Discomfort Association, and the Whirling Dervish Society of Central Arizona, to provide committed moms and dads with a solid background in infant-mobility empathy.

**Cranium Lift:** Lets you empathize with Baby's struggle to raise her disproportionately heavy skull.

1. Lie face down.
2. Ask partner to lightly restrain your arms, and then duct-tape a forty-pound cement block to your head.
3. Raise your skull.
4. To reiterate: *Raise* your skull.

PowerPoint presentation outlining how tummy time prevents developmental delays?

Of course. Have you joined her facedown on the floor so the two of you can languish away the minutes together?

Naturally. Have you attempted to divert her with rattles, picture books, or fantasies of fame and fortune?

Yes! Get to the point! Sorry, your child is not cut out to make her living as a renowned mat-based Pilates instructor. Consider other career paths.

How can I mentor my infant in the art of dashing about? Use your legs as much as possible. Scissor-kick them while resting. Splay them randomly. Stag-leap across parking lots when Baby least expects it. He will soon get the idea.

What if my exhausted legs begin to spasm? Just go with it. Miracles find random muscle contractions engaging.

My partner and I have heard that babies like to "cruise" as a prelude to walking. Having seen Al Pacino's 1980 gay film, *Cruising,* we're concerned. You needn't be. The term "cruising" simply refers to a baby's tendency to hang onto furniture as she staggers determinedly around a room wearing sleazy black leather clothing.

What should parents look for in an infant shoe? As a rule, the younger Baby is, the thinner and more flexible the sole should be. As another rule, avoid gladiator sandals.

How can I tell if my perfect baby will start walking early? By far the best approach is to ask him.

**Goal-Focused Lunge:** Allows you to understand on a profound level the pre-crawler's struggle to reach a desired toy.

1. Visit a designer-shoe warehouse sale.
2. Have partner immobilize your lower-body, then position you five feet from a crazily marked-down pair of Christian Louboutin peep-toe mules.
3. Try to reach shoes before rivals snap them up.

**Imbalance Awareness Drill:** A remarkably effective way to get inside the mind of a wobbly walker.

1. Guzzle seven shots of tequila.
2. Throw back four Merlots.
3. Have partner drizzle crème de menthe into your slack-jawed mouth.
4. Whirl in manner of Whirling Dervish.
5. Go for a little stroll.

# Getting Physical

## THE ADVANTAGES OF A PERSONAL BABY TRAINER

Although miracles get quite a workout merely learning to stand up, it's never too soon to introduce them to the pleasures of regular exercise. You may even want to follow the example of Mia and Peter Boyko of Washington, D.C., one of the growing number of couples who've employed fitness professional to develop their babies' strength, balance, and aerobic skills, thus safeguarding them from the twin specters of underachievement and plus-sized clothing.

Here's a detailed comparison of the leading coaching philosophies, as represented by three of the nation's foremost infant trainers.

### Rolf "Rolfy" Lewis

Philosophy: *Military-inspired.* A former U.S. Army commander, Rolf has been gently pushing infants beyond their limits since 1995. He specializes in disciplined training with an emphasis on groveling.

The Program: Rolf opens each session with brisk combat crawling, then initiates a game of Follow the Leader Through a Harrowing Obstacle Course. Finally, the client is placed in a puddle of putrid Vietnamese mud for intense tummy time.

Fitness Benefits: Increases odds that Baby will survive an imaginary dinosaur attack.

Rules: No insubordination. No conscientious objecting. No novelty hats.

Optional Group Classes: Little Invaders, Aggressive Chanting I & II, and Drop-and-Roll Jazzerobics.

Snacks: Hardtack biscuits. Tepid water. Scavenged berries.

Ideal Clients: Babies who want to learn domination techniques from a master.

## Holly Frenzolli

**Philosophy:** *Play-based.* Holly is a certified baby stimulator with a master's degree in Upbeat Behavioral Psychology. She is 110 percent cheerful, and believes that frantic play is the root of all winning.

**The Program:** The hour begins with five minutes of convulsive laughing, followed by Manic Bubble Popping, Wild Horsey Rides, and Let's Be High-Strung Monkeys. Holly wraps up by urging Baby to perform the splits triumphantly.

**Fitness Benefits:** All clients burn at least ninety calories panting with anxiety.

**Rules:** Every client must be high on life. No exceptions.

**Optional Group Classes:** Cardio Tickling, Risks of Understimulation I & II, and Wanton Destruction.

**Snacks:** Espresso-flavored tofu cubes. Protein goo. Creatine mush.

**Ideal Clients:** Infants who can take a charitable view of Holly's peppiness.

## Leesa P. Leaf

**Philosophy:** *New Age spiritual.* Ms. Leaf subscribes to the view that fitness starts within. As she says, "Only infants in touch with a non-specific higher power can avoid a disastrous body mass index later in life."

**The Program:** First comes a directed visualization in which Baby imagines himself as a ray of brilliant light that is performing jumping jacks. Then Ms. Leaf excuses herself to smoke a cigarette. Finally, she does the baby's numbers.

**Fitness Benefits:** Eventually, you may see a subtle toning of Baby's Chi.

**Rules:** "Just bring your love and your capacity to meditate while I call my broker."

**Optional Group Classes:** Stillness, Neck Consciousness, Low-Impact Blinking, and "How Did I Get So Fat?"

**Snacks:** Whatever ambiguous treats Ms. Leaf can find in her Louis Vuitton tote.

**Ideal Clients:** Out-of-work actor babies and their gullible friends.

# Adventure Travel

## DEALING WITH THE MIRACLE'S MORE RECKLESS URGES

I.

### The Urge to Climb

Though restless miracles typically adore crawling up stairs, they soon discover that tumbling down them is, at best, an acquired taste. You can easily reduce the risks by constructing this unique staircase in your otherwise pointless living room. Inspired by "Ascending and Descending," a 1960 lithograph by the Dutch realist artist M. C. Escher, the staircase conveniently never ends, eliminating both the need to turn around and the threat of discovering a madwoman named Mrs. Rochester at the top. *Bonus:* A centrally located ball pit.

2.

### The Urge to Hover

Perfect babies crave midair experiences and often beg to be shot out of cannons, knowing full well that weapon use is inconsistent with their antiwar stance. Introduce an alternative with this 400-cubic-foot antigravity chamber. Sanitary and fully enclosed, it simulates weightlessness long enough (5.81 seconds) for Baby to perform a single pirouette with no risk of ouchies. Though various side effects can occur (vertigo, farting, light-headedness), at least some of these are reversible upon the miracle's return to earth.

### 3.
### The Urge to Roam

Despite the zero-gravity chamber's appeal, in the end, most miracles prefer to experience life more freely. Since babies are not alley cats, however, it's hardly appropriate to let them skulk unsupervised through the city. Solution: This team of homing swans hoists your child into the skies, allowing him to observe thugs and hos from a safe cruising altitude of fifty feet. Rigorously trained, the no-nonsense birds are conditioned to return Baby to your home after twenty minutes, even if he insists he's really feeling Vegas.

# COME TO DADDY, PLEASE!

### The secret to overcoming developmental plateaus

Sometimes after a string of physical breakthroughs, a perfect baby settles into a slump, claiming to be "over the whole moving thing." If your miracle succumbs to inertia, use the following methods to gently remotivate her:

#### Position an ogre behind Baby

Ideally an ogre who absolutely lives for *Friends* trivia. Your child will soon recall the advantages of mobility.

#### Introduce frequent crawler miles

Make sure Baby understands that once she covers at least .000025 miles, she'll be eligible for a vinyl laptop case.

#### Offer *Price is Right*-style prizes

Even perfect babies will do anything for a pocket calculator, wind chimes, or a grandfather clock.

#### Encase Baby in iron

Then, seating yourself across the room, use a large electromagnet to drag her slowly and compassionately towards you.

**LIGHT-HEARTED**
THE AUDREY HEPBURN SKIP

**PRESIDENTIAL**
THE BILL CLINTON SKIP

# A Walk to Remember

DISTANCE IS ONE THING; STYLE IS
QUITE ANOTHER. HELPING YOUR MIRACLE DEVELOP
A SIGNATURE STRIDE.

When taking their first steps, most average babies are happy to stumble from point A to point B. Miracles, of course, aim higher and generally make it all the way to point K—deftly sidestepping the notoriously vulgar point F.

Merely walking isn't enough, of course. Miracles won't rest until they've mastered a "good walk," which is to say, a trademark gait with a memorable rhythm, as notable as John Travolta's strut in *Saturday Night Fever*, or Princess Diana's gracious amble during her 1991 goodwill tour of Hong Kong.

If your miracle is bumbling about with no particular flair, don't worry: It's not the end of the world. You just have a lazy perfect baby. Follow this four-step plan:

1. **Review the basics:** Any good walk starts with posture. Tell Baby to imagine there is a string attached to the top of her head, held taut by a loving puppeteer named Geppetto who doesn't respect slouchers. Next, make suggestions in a pleasant, sing-song voice: "Shoulders back! Chin up! Butt tight! No, tighter! And walk!" These exhortations should gradually become more and more meaningless: "Work it! Feel the fierce! Too bovine! Angel it up a bit! Give me *cockadoodle*, dammit!"

2. **Study the competition:** While Baby tests out degrees of arm-swing, spy on neighborhood rivals. You'd be surprised what you can learn by peering through basement windows. It's not unheard of to find other miracles attempting to lumber backwards or trot like a Shetland pony.

3. **Select role models carefully:** Take inspiration from famous walkers, but be discriminating. Both *High Noon*'s Gary Cooper and Robocop are timeless choices for boys, but stay away from Foghorn Leghorn (too down-market) and Oscar Wilde (too expressive). Girl babies would do well to emulate Margaret Thatcher or "Mary Richards" in the opening credits of *The Mary Tyler Moore Show*, but not Lassie (too low to the ground). Babies who resist the pressure to conform to gender stereotypes can always focus on the alien in *Alien*.

4. **Add accessories:** Once you've finalized "the walk," take it to the next level with personalized flourishes. Sunglasses create intrigue. Capes add majesty. One Maryland baby blew away the competition by combining a prop crutch with a beatnik finger-snap. Of course, there is such a thing as trying too hard; sometimes, in a sea of stunt-walkers, the most mesmerizing baby of all is standing completely still.

**TWISTING AND SHOUTING**

# Rhythm Methods

Well before he begins nursery school, a perfect baby should be versed in getting his groove on. You'll want to practice dance steps with your miracle in a large, unobstructed area such as a meadow at least five times a week. Choose the program carefully: Not just any two-step or polonaise will do.

| Recommended Dances | Dances to Avoid |
|---|---|
| **CLASSICAL BALLET** <br> *Encourages coltishness.* | **SWORD DANCE** <br> *Lawsuit waiting to happen.* |
| **BELLY DANCING** <br> *Lays the groundwork for a decent six-pack.* | **JAZZ FREESTYLE** <br> *Overuse of "jazz hands" can wreak havoc with computing skills* |
| **THE TANGO** <br> *Lights fire in Baby's soul.* | **THE CAR WASH** <br> *Too menial.* |
| **THE BUMP** <br> *Provides excellent assertiveness training.* | **THE SAILOR'S HORNPIPE** <br> *Nautical dances tend to complicate bath-time.* |
| **THE ROBOT** <br> *Always good for a laugh at Daddy's company picnic.* | **THE CHA-CHA-CHA** <br> *Two chas are acceptable; three are excessive* |

# 7.

## Elevating
# BABY'S MIND

It's crucial to give your miracle every opportunity to learn. Imagine if Baby became a bore just because you failed to provide an ample assortment of educational toys, books, and mobiles. Not to mention, a decent tapestry loom and—if at all possible—her own Guatemalan volcano with a stable observation deck. If you lack any of these, buy them now. We'll wait . . .

Finished? Terrific.

That said, the most important learning tool you can offer Baby is you. Elevating her mind is not a simple matter of plunking her down before a Central American volcano with an endless supply of notepaper while you wander off. The truth of the matter is that notepaper, in and of itself, isn't that edifying.

Fortunately, getting involved in your child's mental growth doesn't require a major time commitment. An average session of stimulation involves no more than a little reading aloud and some rhythmic clapping, plus a minute or two to demystify crop-circles, name everyday objects, selectively breed legumes, deliver a calf, make funny faces, choose tapestry wool in authentic pre-Raphaelite colors, construct a geodesic dome, glare at an uncooperative volcano, replicate the nesting habits of the snowy owl, and—assuming Baby is still itching for knowledge—solve for x.

Keep it light and fun. Never pressure your miracle. If his attention wanders, do not point out that *some* daydreamers end up sleeping on *hide-a-beds* in cramped apartments with *transsexual porn stars* for neighbors. Such remarks are hardly proactive.

Should Baby continue to show more interest in the ceiling than in his stacking toys, however, you might want to casually allude to the cutthroat world of nursery school or leave a highlighted copy of Darwin's *The Origins of Species* in his crib, so he can absorb the "survival of the fittest" concept at a relaxed pace in a comfortable setting.

In the end, the key to successfully

# Are You Boring Your Miracle?

## DON'T MISS THESE SUBTLE SIGNS OF UNDERSTIMULATION

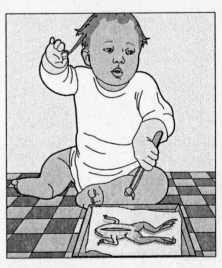

### Baby displays foot-restlessness

Although this infant is successfully operating an interactive toy switchboard, she's clearly unchallenged by the relentless call volume. Observe how she's absentmindedly "drawing circles" with her shoe. Unless her parents intervene soon, this baby will never learn the country code for Thailand.

**If this happens to your child:** Engage her by ornamenting the switchboard with mirrors and crinkle paper.

### Baby plays idly with hair

Hair-twirling always indicates that a miracle's educational program lacks something. The frog this infant has been given to dissect, for instance, is obviously leaving her cold—perhaps because neither it nor its internal organs are beloved animated characters trademarked by a large multi-national corporation.

**If this happens to your child:** Give Baby something more intriguing to disembowel, such as a Dissect-Me Elmo.

stimulating your miracle's mind is finding a balance. Go ahead and invest in an educational volcano, but don't confuse it with a caring tutor. Make funny faces, but not hysterically funny faces. And never persist in singing seventeenth-century madrigals if Baby displays signs of overstimulation. You'll know he has reached his limit if he averts his gaze, begins to whimper, or reviews your performance negatively for the *New York Times*.

As painful as such feedback can be, it's still safer to overwhelm Baby than to underwhelm him. To avoid that catastrophe, study the following guidelines until you glaze over.

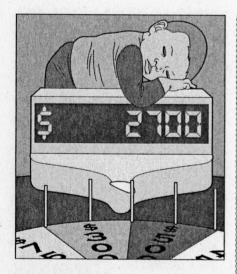

### Baby conks out

While it's possible that this young contestant on "Wheel of Fortune" is contemplating whether or not to buy a vowel, it's more likely that the tedious task of spelling out the answer to the "Rhyme Time" puzzle has lulled him to sleep. At this point, his chances of winning the deluxe, forty-eight-foot motor home are nil.

**If this happens to your child:** Call his agent immediately and insist she book him on the more challenging "Jeopardy."

## SIZING UP THE COMPETITION

As child psychologists have come to understand what constitutes "genius" in more nuanced ways, IQ rankings have been revised accordingly:

| IQ | Level of Intelligence |
| --- | --- |
| 110 | Apprentice Genius |
| 115 | Entry-Level Genius |
| 120 | Associate Genius |
| 125 | Senior Associate Genius |
| 128 | Deputy Genius |
| 130 | Genius |
| 131+ | VP in charge of Genius |

Source: The American Institute of IQ Inflation

**Strike a balance when stimulating your child's mind: It's safe to make funny faces, but never expose him to hysterically funny faces.**

# Strings Attached

## THE SEVEN CRUCIAL CRIB MOBILES

Although anthropologists have noted that primitive man survived without mobiles—was it simply too tricky to clamp them onto Baby's cave walls?—most experts argue that modern infants require at least eleven developmentally appropriate models. How ridiculous: You really only need these seven.

**1.**
### Solid Earthly Values Mobile

This breakthrough in infant psychology, consists of a large, fresh potato that parents must replace every three days. As it bobs provocatively, it instills in Baby an appreciation of nature's bounty, a respect for bobbing things, and a lifelong fear of carbs.

**2.**
### Attainable Goals Mobile

Icons representing easily reachable, non-threatening artistic goals—an Oscar, an Emmy, a Grammy—hang casually just out of Baby's reach. If your infant dismisses these ambitions as too mundane, upgrade to the Nobel/Pulitzer model to silence him.

**3.**
### Motivational Speakers Mobile

Wind up this charmer and its little orators start ranting at Baby inspiringly, urging her to get her life together, overcome her objections to rolling over, cut her debt load, master real estate in her spare time, and figure out how to hold a raisin.

**4.**
### Classic Dust Mobile

Specks of organic soil dance and gambol in the air like miniature Baryshnikovs, training Baby's vision to focus on details. This will benefit him later whether he's serving as a professional assassin or setting a festive table.

## MOBILES THAT CANNOT, IN GOOD FAITH, BE RECOMMENDED

The Sistine Chapel Ceiling Mobile (actual size): *Too bulky.*
Mobile, Alabama, Mobile: *Too predictable.*
The Immobile Mobile: *Too subtle.*
The Funny Bunnies Mobile: *Insufficiently funny.*

**5.**

### World of Pasta Varieties Mobile

In the future, when Baby's nursery school peers are loafing about disputing the merits of vermicelli versus tagliarini or making cruel gemelli puns, she'll have no need to hang her head in shame, thanks to this instructive, lightly salted mobile.

**6.**

### Scary Germanic High-Contrast Mobile

This teaches Baby to see the world in black and white and also to celebrate Oktoberfest. It may make Baby cry, but you must be firm.

**7.**

### Dangers of Smoking Mobile

Two sets of lungs—one healthy, the other shriveled and cancerous—rotate to the familiar strains of "Old McDonald Had a Four-Pack-a-Day Habit." You aren't forbidding Baby to smoke; you're simply laying out the choices.

# Perfect Literacy
## THE ABCS OF READING TO YOUR MIRACLE

**A** *is for* **as soon as possible**
Start reading aloud to Baby early; ideally during conception.

**B** *is for* **bewitching**
Mesmerize your infant's senses with books that make amusing sounds, feature fuzzy textures, or smell like a wet afternoon on the banks of the Hudson in 1701.

**C** *is for* **cozy**
Cuddle your child to make sure he associates reading with pleasure. This will help him master a key college-age skill: the ability to finish Beowulf while making out with Zoe Weber.

**D** *is for* **demanding**
Challenge Baby with enriched books such as *The Lengthy-German-Word Primer*, in which "A is for Adventskranzkerzenan-zünder" (advent wreath candlelighter) and "B is for Betäubungs mittelverschreibungsverordnung" (you don't want to know).

**E** *is for* **echo effect**
Choose books that feature repetition. Then, just to be safe, repeat each word eleven times.

**F** *is for* **fun**
Make silly expressions as you read, pretend to be surprised by twist endings, and remember: Few things delight miracles more than a really vibrant index.

**G** *is for* **glamorous**
Before you read a single word, make sure that both you and your child are stylishly, yet soberly, dressed.

**H** *is for* **hidden agendas**
Beware corrupting messages buried in classic texts. It's become clear, for instance, that Thing One and Thing Two in The Cat in the Hat were originally named Gomorrah and Sodom.

**I** *is for* **interaction**
Pause frequently to ask Baby questions about the pictures. For example: "Can you see the orphan whose intrinsic goodness allows him to triumph over both cruelty and corruption? Yes, there he is! What a pretty Oliver Twist!"

**J** *is for* **juicy**
At first, the miracle regards any book less as an intellectual adventure and more as a chewy appetizer. Keep an array of exotic condiments and chutneys handy to make sure she's feasting memorably.

**K** *is for* **knowing glances**
Look for books that depict objects Baby finds familiar. Miracles love to point at things they value, such as the architecture of Brasília.

**L** *is for* **lip-synching**
Sooner or later, most parents ask themselves, "Would Baby learn more if I merely mouthed words that have been prerecorded by Shakespearean actors with superior enunciation and great accents?" This is, of course, a very personal decision.

For M through Z, please send $10,000 and a stamped, self-addressed envelope to: "Pardon Me, But Where Are the Rest of My Tips?" c/o *The Perfect Baby Handbook*, 175 Michaelmas Place, New York City, NY, 10016

---

A POINT TO PONDER

**"The baby who deserves the most pity is the lonesome one on a rainy day who doesn't know how to read—and is subsequently reduced to playing hilarious pranks on his Puritan mama."**
—*Benjamin Franklin, Age 3, 1709*

# The Tale of a Fierce, Bad Drawing

No matter how well written a children's book may be, it can't promote intelligence adequately if it's poorly illustrated. Compare the subtle but significant gap in quality between these two seemingly interchangeable images.

**A GOOD ILLUSTRATION**
This timeless drawing displays all the hallmarks of stimulating work: a whimsical line, recognizable subjects, and a strategic balance between simple and complex shapes.

**A BAD ILLUSTRATION**
This drawing is less thoughtfully rendered. Note the muddy colors, odd proportions, and excessive detail—not to mention the clumsy depiction of bird vomit.

---

## GOOD RIDDANCE, MOON

**Reading Baby your favorite childhood books would be a lovely rite of passage if she found them less dull. Luckily, more stimulating versions are now available:**

| ORIGINAL TITLE | ENRICHED EDITION |
| --- | --- |
| Make Way for Ducklings | Make Way for Duckling L'Orange |
| Curious George | Freudian George |
| Go, Dog, Go! | Proceed, Labradoodle, Proceed! |
| Hop on Pop | Mount the Patriarch |
| One Fish, Two Fish | A Heartbreaking Array of |
| Red Fish, Blue Fish | Staggeringly Numerous Fish |
| Pat the Bunny | Pat the Great Gatsby |
| Horton Hears a Who! | Horton Hears a Whence! |

# Six Degrees of Stimulation

## QUESTIONS TO ASK YOURSELF WHEN
## CHOOSING A CUTTING-EDGE EDUCATIONAL TOY

### I.
### Does the plaything resemble an overweight monkey?

Toys based on obese animals have large, easily identifiable faces—a key factor in engaging Baby's attention and her pity.

### 2.
### Does it combine garish colors and unsettling patterns?

Baby reacts most strongly to toys that seem to have been designed by insane Japanese schoolgirls who've had too much coffee.

### 3.
### Is the toy a feast of provocative textures?

Does it invite tactile exploration by combining the tickle of feathers, the pointiness of pinecones, and the bumpiness of a skin condition?

### 4.
### Can Baby interact with it?

Does it feature peekaboo eye flaps? Buttons that make it squeak or explode? Can your child use it to grate cheese or dial the Netherlands?

### 5.
### Does it perform a light show that recalls a 1992 Def Leppard concert?

Your miracle can't help but respond to playthings that shoot piercing beams of light into her eyes.

### 6.
### Is it festooned with mirrors?

Mirrors help Baby form facial expressions that convincingly suggest she *loves* the toy. She doesn't want to hurt your feelings, after all.

# Teasing Baby's Brain

## HOW TO CHALLENGE YOUR GROWING MIRACLE WITH SILLY PUZZLES AND GRUELING GAMES

Some parents assume their child won't want to play with them just because they lack brightly patterned skin and don't stack well. They needn't worry. As long as you know a few mentally invigorating games, your baby will often choose you over his toys. Here are some favorites to explore:

**Facial contortion games:** Next time you're diapering your child, shape your mouth into the letter O and watch his eyes light up. If you're feeling confident in the pliability of your lips, attempt to form the plus sign (+), the ampersand (&), or the entire Hebrew alphabet.

**Hand-based fun:** Slightly older miracles are ready for clapping games such as Patty Cake and If You're the Reincarnation of Kurt Cobain, Only Happy, and You Know It, Clap Your Hands!

**Mimicry games:** Start with a simple head roll, pausing to let your infant imitate you. Progress to a challenging Jersey accent; Baby will repeat your words flawlessly. Continue in this vein for three minutes, then say, "Okay, now let's stop imitating Mommy," followed by, "I mean it," followed by, "No, seriously, please," followed by a tension headache.

**Inside versus outside games:** Encourage your miracle to crawl through a plastic tunnel or a spandex tube-dress from 1988. The sensation of being "in" and then suddenly "out" will help prepare her for the possibility of fleeting fame.

**Object-permanence challenges:** Games like Peek-a-Book, which teach infants that objects continue to exist even when they can't see them, are thrilling as long as you raise the stakes for more mature babies.

Amanda and Kit Nelson, of Rancho Palos Verdes, California, hired magician David Copperfield to make their entire gated community disappear—though only after he guaranteed them in writing that he'd reinstate it before bedtime.

**Language activities:** Riddles and rhymes are always fun, but nothing engages miracles as thoroughly as crossword puzzles. Infants older than 12 months may insist on holding the pencil. In such cases, propose a trade-off. Make it clear you'll allow this if Baby stops rolling her eyes every time the solution is "aura," "aria," "eon," or "obi."

# Disc Management

AVOID "EDUCATIONAL" DVDS—EXCEPT, OF COURSE, THOSE CREATED BY OTHER PERFECT BABIES

Though it's tempting to buy your miracle DVDs such as *Baby Genius: Left Brain Stimulation* or its sequel *No, A Little to the Right*, resist the impulse. Studies have suggested that these discs can stunt your infant's vocabulary and leave him with an asymmetrical head.

Instead, seek out instructional DVDs that have been designed and programmed by perfect babies themselves. With titles like *Moving Past Velcro* and *So, You Want to Be a Sleeper?*, they focus on practical issues that really matter to your child. A detailed guide to three of the best:

### Negotiating with Cats

*Created by Pinnacle Rose Trylowsky, age 15 months*

Confronts an ugly truth no adult DVD maker has had the courage to face: *Cats hate perfect babies.* The fearless Ms. Trylowsky presents a structured workshop that trains miracles to bargain successfully with vengeful calicos, bitchy Persians, and the immoral Siamese.

**Special Features:** A bonus section called Establishing Territories provides persuasive talking points ("Okay, Inky, you can have the dusty top of the dining room buffet if I get the entire kitchen").

**Flaws:** Completely overlooks the menace of kittens. A poorly lit scene in which a tabby lures a baby inside a steamer trunk seems unnecessarily sensationalized.

**Production Values:** Surprisingly good, considering that Ms. Trylowsky shot her footage while under constant attack by two Brazilian shorthairs.

**Bottom Line:** A winner. Practical, unsentimental tactics from a baby who's been there. No other DVD teaches interspecies communcation skills as well, except perhaps for Trylowsky's follow-up effort, *Sweet-Talking Dingos.*

## Getting Through a Playdate
*Created by Northam Teetle, age 12 months*

After his indiscriminate parents scheduled 142 playdates for him over a six-month period, Mr. Teetle felt he was uniquely qualified to outline the challenges of forced intimacy on kitchen floors. Judging from this DVD's glowing Amazon.com reviews, countless babies agree.

**Special Features:** An in-depth section on blind playdates covers such topics as Hitting the Jackpot, Tactful Rejection Tips, and The Occasional Need to Throw Up on Your Date.

**Flaws:** In hindsight, Mr. Teetle's decision to cast his father as a baby in some of *Getting Through a Playdate*'s dramatic reenactments was probably a mistake.

**Production Values:** Strong all round. The costume consultant deserves a special shout-out for squeezing Mr. Teetle's dad into a size 4 onesie.

**Bottom Line:** Both frank and encouraging. Despite its flaws, this breakthrough title has helped miracles everywhere continue their search for kindred playmates with a little more diplomacy and a little less spastic outrage.

## An Omnibus of Parent Bloopers
*Compiled by A. J. and J. A. Williams*

Features more than seventy amateur video clips of hilariously overwhelmed parents—ranging from a dad who inadvertently diapers his own head to a mom who becomes entangled in her Balinese baby-wearing cloth and tumbles down a gentle hill.

**Special Features:** The Williams twins outdo themselves with a rare collection of Royal Parent Bloopers, featuring Queen Helena-Astrid of Norway utterly failing to master a breast pump.

**Flaws:** The Drunk Parent Bloopers section settles for easy laughs (a sloshed father falling off a Dutch rocking horse, a tipsy mommy fleeing a giant bubble).

**Production Values:** Expertly edited and sensitively scored with Brahms classics. Certain clips, however, obviously shot by sleepy newborns, are blurry and unrewarding.

**Bottom Line:** Highly recommended. Though the Norwegian royal family has officially denounced this DVD, it effectively uses humor to introduce key concepts like vulnerability and the dangers of rocking under the influence.

# Kicking It Old School
## TRADITIONAL TOYS
### FROM SIMPLER, DULLER ERAS

The infant "edutainment" industry has long faced charges that its pricey computerized teaching toys do nothing but exploit parents' fears. Now research is suggesting that playthings that digitally beep, sing, squawk, or deliver Alec Baldwin's monologue from *Glengarry Glen Ross* also dangerously raise the odds that Baby will pursue theater studies in central Florida.

Understandably, parents are worried. Turning their backs on technology, they are embracing simple, "back-to-basics" toys that in many cases just sit there— ingeniously forcing Baby to stimulate herself. The seven top sellers:

1. **Lump of Wax on a Stick** Once all the rage in ancient Rome, this primitive doll (around $90) may not impress Baby immediately. Enthusiastic parents are reporting, however, that their children become transfixed when this object abruptly melts in August.

2. **Dirt** A remnant of a more innocent time, this vintage toy (price varies) occasionally shows up on eBay. Parents claim that infants can use it to create shapes and apparently prefer this to watching computer-animated shapes dance a minuet.

3. **Dried Gourd Rattle** Common in the Middle Ages, vegetable-based rattles ($70-$180) have never been proven to raise a baby's IQ. Still, one or two of the geniuses who designed the great medieval cathedrals might possibly have shaken them. Coincidence?

4. **Introductory Banter Kit** The idea that two infants could mutually profit from chitchat first emerged in the 1920s. Though this activity kit ($258) does not specifically teach counting or colors, it delivers other benefits, equipping Baby, for instance, to flourish in the bar scene.

5. **Cardboard Box** Consider springing for a deluxe model ($78) even if your miracle gravitates toward some dusty old box in your basement. While both versions have movable flaps and can be crawled into, only premium boxes can be crawled *out of*.

6. **Grandpa's Hair** A sharp pull on this toy (price negotiable) elicits grunts, yelps, and stimulating expressions like "Ooof!"

7. **Traditional Rag™** This replica of a classic Great Depression toy ($138) is sometimes marketed as Worthless Scrap of Cloth. At first, most babies prod the Rag™ uncertainly, attempting to make it light up. When that fails, they shove it into their computer drives and click "play." Eventually, the emergency computer repairman arrives and demands $500 an hour, exposing infants to important lessons about extortion.

# The Payoffs of Stimulation
### THANK-YOU E-MAILS
### FROM SATISFIED MIRACLES

**Hey, Mom and Dad,**

Thank you, thank you for devoting so much time to my intellectual development. I am now an intellectual. My only regrets are that I'm arguably humorless and bad at sports, except triathlon.

*Rebecca F. Esterhazy, age 9*

**Dear Dad,**

It's a good thing you drilled me on the Periodic Table of the Elements when I was little, cuz this weird thing just happened after school. Manganese (#25) and Argon (#18) ganged up on me and started shoving me around—but, thanks to you and Helium (#2), I knew exactly what to do.

*Theo P. Purves, age 7*

**Dear Mother,**

Although I was resistant at the time, I've come to realize how wise you were to dress me in educational medieval armor as a toddler. Incidentally, I am thriving at King Arthur Jousting Camp this summer and will see you anon.

*Susannah Esmé Chen, age 9*

**Hey, you two,**

Remember how you only let me play with gender-neutral toys? Well, guess what? My class just voted me "Most Gender Neutral Freshman"! I can't believe I beat out both Blair Aesop Stevens *and* Quinn Peyton Davis.

*Morgan Langley Gray, age 14*

**Hey Olive and Gaspard,**

You guys did a fricking amazing job on my brain. It kicks ass! Is it true that Nanny Schwartz is back with the Marines?

*Camille Turgeon, age 9*

**Dear Mommy and Daddy,**

Was it only 10 years ago that we explored the prehistoric cave drawings at Lascaux? I think of those times whenever my friends complement me on the clothes I sew myself from the skins of large carnivorous animals.

*Dieter Franz Jones, age 10½*

**Dear Mama,**

Thank you for training me to serve canapes correctly. It's a good skill to fall back on if all my think-tank dreams fizzle.

*Samuel Jacobs, age 6*

# 8.

## Flawless
# STYLE

**P**erfect baby clothing must be sensible. It's hard work being miraculous, and purely frivolous style is just not appropriate. Even a novelty T-shirt, for instance, should boast a functioning neck hole, unless Baby's made it clear she plans to wear it as a headscarf while sculpting. So shop carefully. To ensure the item is practical in every sense of the word, ask yourself the following questions:

**Is the garment comfortable?** Stiff Nehru collars and overly elasticized waistbands repress Baby's creativity. No miracle wants to feel cinched into his or her clothing unless it's Victorian Corset Day at daycare.

**Is it too comfortable?** Excessively loose clothing, on the other hand, can lead to laziness, out-of-body experiences, and overuse of the phrase "slouchy seventies style."

**Is the fabric durable?** While heavy-duty cotton is always a good choice, some of the best new baby clothes are being manufactured in Japan out of light-gauge copper.

**Is the item cozy enough?** Say it's a pair of corduroy overalls. Ask yourself: Would a hairless Chihuahua covet these overalls on a chilly night in Michigan? If you're unsure, ask the clerk if it's possible to see the overalls in a four-legged version.

**Is it too cozy?** Avoid overly warm, sleep-inducing garments. Miracles must remain alert at all times except during regularly scheduled naps.

**Is it one of the four acceptable baby colors—which is to say, a pale shade of pink, blue, yellow, or green?** If not, it's entirely possible that you're purchasing an impractical item such as a Caribbean vacation or a 65" flat-screen TV.

**Does the item inflate in emergencies?** This mainly applies to walking shoes.

**Is it likely to fit for more than a week?** Such pieces are enormously practical for babies who can afford to be seen at the park in the same outfit twice.

**Will the garment help you simplify the dressing process?** Items with snaps or Velcro closures are by far the most efficient. If you're an unusually dexterous parent, however, a case can be made for tiny, exquisite seed-pearl buttons.

**Is it French?** The practical advantage of French-made clothing is that it comes with a complimentary croissant.

**Has a celebrity baby ever worn the item?** Don't get too alarmed. Even previously used clothing may still be suitable for your miracle if you wash it in hot water immediately.

**Is there any way you could laboriously hand-smock at least part of the garment?** These items save you the trouble of scouring Ecuador for more authentically detailed pieces.

**Is it made of the palest Venetian linen?** Such garments are especially practical for perfect babies who prefer to lie absolutely still in sanitized environments and watch the minutes slowly tick by.

**Is it a puffy fairy skirt that includes a set of sparkly wings?** Should be fine as long as the wings are compliant with federal aviation regulations.

**Is it a humorous sweatshirt that identifies Baby as "Unemployed"?** Extremely practical if Baby has recently stepped down from the board of directors at Baby Gap. Otherwise not.

**Does it feature exactly twenty-four colorful wool tassels?** As you'll discover, there's really no other way to bring the educational concept of "two dozen" to life.

**Is the item dry-clean only?** This requirement is always preferable to hand-wash-by-grumpy-nanny-who-is-threatening-to-quit only.

**Is it a size 1 opera slipper?** Highly practical. Especially if there are two of them.

---

A POINT TO PONDER

# "Common sense ain't common."

*—Cherokee-American cowboy, actor, and social commentator Will Rogers,*
*age 16 months, after an upsetting encounter with a poorly constructed pair of infant chaps.*

# The Cuteness Question

### PRACTICALITY ASIDE, BABY OUTFITS MUST ALSO ACHIEVE AN APPROPRIATE LEVEL OF ADORABILITY. AVOID THESE RISKY EXTREMES.

### Too Cute

Elspeth's ensemble appears to be a festive look that's gone astray. The problem is subtle, but perhaps you can spot it. That's right: the footwear. Baby shoes that incorporate jack-in-the-boxes can easily cross the line from cute to creepy. **Elspeth's parents respond:** "Oh, God . . . really? Our hope was that the jack-in-the-box effect would symbolize the way Elspeth is constantly bursting with joy. So . . . that didn't come across at all?"

### Insufficiently Cute

On the other hand, Dalton's minimalist look is overly grim. A poncho is a bold choice, but it needn't echo the shape of Mount Fuji quite so rigidly unless Baby is Japanese. (That gloomy shade of eel-gray isn't helping.) Meanwhile, Dalton's severe glasses and oversized statement ring seem more appropriate for an annoying world-class architect than a child. **Dalton's parents respond:** "As world-class architects, we naturally disagree."

# Improving on Perfection

## TACKLING THE THREE
## MOST COMMON MAKEOVER CHALLENGES
## MIRACLES FACE TODAY

### I. Dressing Age-Appropriately

**BEFORE:** Lachlan, age 11 months, is dressing too young. It's no wonder his music teacher doesn't take him seriously. The shortie tee, Goth wristband, and shark's tooth necklace all suggest a naïve delinquent whose ambitions are limited to dealing meth. When you factor in the ungroomed hair and the babyish novelty socks, Lachlan is pretty much the last person you'd trust to perform Brahms's violin concerto in D major.

**AFTER:** With a few tweaks, Lachlan's style takes on a more sophisticated, yet still youthful vibe. While a herringbone-weave sweater introduces a note of gravitas, the cocky accent scarf instantly telegraphs that Lachlan is not some stodgy old fart. A Pasotti duck-head umbrella, Tod's driving shoes (in tan), and a more professional hairstyle make it clear that Lachlan would never nap his way through an orchestral cue.

As much as perfect babies would love to wear skinny jeans or experiment with "the new volume," it's just not possible. When you have a squat, oddly proportioned body, many styles are off limits. Trench coats don't work. Suspenders can pinch during tummy time. Droopy dolman sleeves rob you of what little elbow you have. Luckily, for every problem there is a makeover.

## 2. Dealing with Figure Flaws

 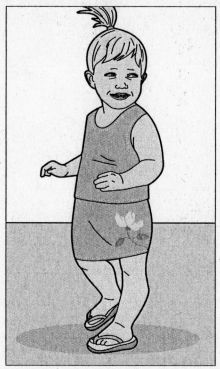

**BEFORE:** Like many babies, Mia is on the short side, but misguided wardrobe choices are making her seem even stubbier. In a flared skirt, bloated leg-o'-mutton sleeves, and horizontal stripes, Mia looks more like a doublewide mobile home than an infant. Unflattering rubber boots chop her legs off at midcalf and, while it's unclear who chose to emphasize Mia's necklessness with a retro 1950s scarf, it was an unloving decision.

**AFTER:** With a sleeker, simplified look, Mia suddenly appears at least thirty-three inches tall. A monochromatic color scheme lengthens her lines and makes her giggle at her own elegance. A crisply tailored skirt erases diaper bulge while a scoop tee creates the illusion of a bona fide neck. Also elongating: a sprightly updo and flesh-toned sandals that make Mia's legs appear to go on for minutes and minutes.

## 3. Going from Day to Night

**BEFORE:** Although Bethany's daytime look is ideal for a boring afternoon of rejecting toys at emergency daycare, she's hardly ready to zip to a 7:00 p.m. gallery opening with her intimidatingly cosmopolitan mom. The brown sweater, while snuggly, is too reminiscent of dull indigenous tribes to wow the sort of people who take appropriations of Marlboro ads seriously as art. Her mundane romper, with its prim Peter Pan collar, also falls short of chic.

**AFTER:** With some swift subtractions and a few additions, Bethany is ready to face the culture vultures. She's been encouraged to ditch the sweater, roll up her romper's sleeves, and flip the collar for a rocker vibe that's more urban, less aboriginal. Despite ten minutes of outraged protest, she has submitted to a statement belt and allowed her hair to be gelled into a spiky neo-eighties 'do. To cap off the edgy look, she has drooled asymmetrically.

---

## WORDS TO DRESS BY

### Inspire Baby with timeless advice from infant-style guru Diana Vreeland

"Always wear your bib back-to-front; it is so much more flattering." *(1949)*

"Tie black velvet bows on your ears to look like you have bigger ears." *(1956)*

"For a brisk crawl in Monaco, the only inspired choice is chiffon." *(1961)*

"Elegance is innate. It has nothing to do with being over two feet tall." *(1967)*

# Unnecessary Evils

## THE THIN LINE BETWEEN
## "CUTE" AND "CRUEL" BABY HATS

Infants can make almost anything look cute. Of a wool cap crafted to resemble a bulbous eggplant, one dad was overheard to say: "It's obnoxious! In that 'only babies can pull it off' way! Let's see what my little guy can do with this one!"

This is insensitive parenting. No miracle can maintain his composure in a eggplant hat for long without worrying that some undiscerning vegan will try to eat his head. And yet, the production of this and other equally abusive baby hats continues with no restrictions. As a concerned parent, you have two options: Agitate for laws that require craft stores to run mental health checks before selling colorful wool, or observe the following dos and don'ts.

**Do** stick to a canvas bucket hat, a plain wool cap, or any hat that was personally crocheted by a relative with a generous will.

**Do** make exceptions for boring newborns who could desperately use a little jazzing up.

**Don't** buy anything else—to be specific:

· Your baby's head should not resemble a tomato, a berry, a brussel sprout, a delicious dessert, or a roast chicken with drumsticks.

· Neither should it evoke the Lincoln Memorial, a "mad cow," or 1940s swimming sensation Esther Williams' bathing cap.

· Antennae are compromising.

· Peruvians make mistakes too.

· Jingle bells can screw up Baby's efforts to meditate.

· Unless Baby has enemies who need to be gored, resist any hat equipped with horns.

· Court jesters were not respected members of society.

· Tiny replicas of Queen Elizabeth's hats really only work when Baby is christening ships.

· Avoid hats that, as one Mom put it, "give kids the idea that the world is full of friendly people because everyone they meet starts cracking up."

*fig.1*

**REGRETTABLE**
THE VIKING HAT

**DRIPPY**
THE SUNDAE HAT

# The Stylish Life

## A MIRACLE'S GUIDE TO THE SOCIAL GRACES

To be truly stylish, a perfect baby must master etiquette and also spend a couple of minutes a day on decorum. He should know how to eat in public, enter a room, and be conversant, at least on a grunting level, in subjects ranging from napping to international horsemanship. Do not stint in this area: As the old saying goes, you can dress a perfect baby up, but you can't always take him to your judgmental friend Sabrina's house.

## The Niceties of Toy Sharing

Certain infants lack manners, forcing you to pry Mr. Potato Head gently from their claw-like hands. Make sure your own baby knows the rules:

1. **Any request to share should be obliged within five minutes:** It's acceptable, however, for Baby to ruin the toy first through vigorous, investigative play.
2. **Beady-eyed expressions are discouraged:** Your miracle may be tempted to dart hostile glances at covetous babies. Remind him that this photographs poorly.
3. **After one baby lends another a toy, it's customary to send a handwritten thank-you note:** Or burp in the sharer's face. Either is fine.

---

## MAKING AN ENTRANCE

You'll know you've trained Baby to crawl into a crowded room correctly when everyone present sits up, takes notice, and tingles (in that order). A few tips:

**Urge Baby to relax her facial muscles:** Before she begins her entrance, massage her features lightly. Pursed lips or an overly clenched jaw can ruin everything.

**Suggest she pause in the doorway for effect:** As the door frames her, Baby should lift one hand off the floor and make a sweeping gesture as if to say, "And what have we here?" Remind her to survey the room: Baby should regard her guests slowly and graciously, smiling a bit more broadly when she recognizes Grandma.

**Prod her to enter the room:** As she crawls forward, Baby should stop and confer briefly with some guests, but not others, creating a sense of exclusivity.

**Don't be surprised when Baby falls asleep on a guest's handbag:** Baby is exhausted.

# Getting a Grip

Any self-respecting miracle should learn how navigate the silverware at a formal White House dinner. A piece-by-piece guide:

**Seafood fork**
To be tossed over shoulder, accidentally stabbing a pharmaceuticals lobbyist.

**Catapulter Utensil**
Essential for all mashed foods that might improve the State Dining Room's wallpaper.

**Dessert spoon**
To be left resentfully untouched. (Mommy discourages sugar.)

**Soup spoon**
For catching a glimpse of self and becoming transfixed, thus evading nosy questions from an Idaho senator's wife.

**Dinner fork**
For chasing peas suspensefully.

**Salad fork**
For transferring Boston Bibb lettuce leaves to top of head for an adorable photo op.

**Unsafe knife**
To be thrown to the floor in disgust.

**Melon spoon**
To be brandished while making a forceful point about daycare standards.

A POINT TO PONDER

**"Babies who have mastered etiquette, who are entirely, impeccably right, would seem to arrive at a point of exquisite dullness. If you reach this juncture, poo on your napkin."**

—*Dorothy Parker, Age 3, 1896*

# Nurturing Attire

YOUR OWN CLOTHING CAN BE A POWERFUL CHILD-REARING TOOL—IF YOU CHOOSE IT CAREFULLY

S tudy after study has proven that you can parent most effectively in dowdy or outlandish outfits that reassure Baby you're putting him first. Ignore this basic rule and you may have a problem on your hands.

When Los Angeles couple Sandra and Alexi Koziak persisted in wearing flattering Armani separates, their daughter, Lola, naturally concluded that their parental duties had slipped their minds. She decided to stage an intervention, subjecting her mom and dad to three hours of tough-love techniques (at one point, shredding a valuable accordian-pleated skirt).

Though Lola finally persuaded the Koziaks to invest in shapeless sweats, they could have spared themselves and their daughter needless trauma if they'd done their homework. Consider these more loving approaches.

*fig. 1*

### The Educational Look

The crucial 0 to 3 month period is no time for restrained tweeds or florals. Research has revealed that black-and-white patterns stimulate newborns most effectively, so stock up on pieces like this "Attentive-Harlequin Suit" from L.A. design team Loud and Unsettling. To underline your commitment to Baby, accessorize with a dirty diaper.

fig. 2

fig. 3

### The Selfless, Unraveled Look

Communicate your willingness to sacrifice style by wearing any rag within arm's reach. This mother has pulled on a stretched-out tee, coordinated it with a frayed sweater, then recklessly knotted a soggy bath towel at her waist. She has taken extra care to ground the outfit with mismatched gym socks and graceless plastic shoes.

### The Subtly Prideful Look

When going out on the town, reinforce Baby's importance with clothing that's been custom-printed with images of her face. Don't overdo it or Baby may grow self-conscious and completely change her hairdo, rendering herself unrecognizable. This couple has limited themselves to a few select pieces, plus a personalized helium balloon.

# Groomed for Success

## MAKE THE MOST OF YOUR BABY'S CROWNING GLORY, WHETHER IT CONSISTS OF SIX OR 6000 HAIRS

### The New Shag

If your newborn feels her hair is too thin and lifeless, try a variation on stylist Sally Hershberger's renowned "shag," aiming for graduated layers that shift and shimmer.

### The Thug

Don't embarrass an edgy newborn by gelling his few strands into a pitiful faux Mohawk. Wiglets, like these mutton-chop "sideburns," deliver a more convincingly threatening look.

### The Competitor

Plentiful hair is not an advantage in and of itself. Give Baby a truly stand-out look by braiding her tresses into an approximation of the Olympic rings, topped with a modest bow.

### The Wolfgang

A traditional style that still works some attitude, this style (based on a rare portrait of the youthful Mozart) updates a classic look with a beaded Rasta braid.

### The Babar

If your miracle wants to showcase her hair's natural volume, hire a professional landscaper to sculpt it until it resembles a topiary elephant happily extending its trunk.

### The Bohemian

A baby blessed with abundant hair often resists grooming interference. Back off and enjoy the creative way he accessorizes his mane by rolling in debris.

# 9.

## Communicating with
# BABY

Understandably, you're eager to start chatting with Baby as soon as possible. Nothing brings parent and child closer, after all, than a heart-to-heart discussion like those featured in the legendary chick-flick *Beaches*. (Note: Traditionally, Baby tackles the free-spirited Bette Midler role, while Mommy or Daddy must content themselves with the long-suffering Barbara Hershey part.)

You need to be patient, however. Baby is in no position to share her overwrought relationship concerns with you over a piece of cheesecake—or to sympathize with yours—until she actually learns to speak. And that can take days, even months.

Though some miracles talk implausibly early, others feel they have nothing material to say until well after their second birthdays, opting to exceed expectations in other ways. Verbal delays can be troubling, but whichever path your infant chooses, make sure you react appropriately.

**If your offspring shows no interest in talking:** Focus on the positives. Remember that miracles can and do communicate in all kinds of other ways: through body language, by crying, and by crumpling up flashcards and flinging them to the ground. Once you learn to overinterpret these nonverbal cues, they're fascinating.

If Baby is still not talking after 18 months, there may be cause for concern. After consulting a pediatric speech therapist, Beth and Tim Moss, a quietly intense Toronto couple, finally grasped that their infant had mistaken them for Trappist monks and taken a vow of contemplative silence. More often than not, Baby is

## Don't expect Baby to critique your parenting skills right away. His insights may be limited to "dodo" and "umph."

exploring language privately, perhaps through the practice of journaling, and faces no real developmental danger. Successful late talkers include David Letterman, Johnny Carson, and Conan O'Brien.

**If your miracle begins sighing expressively during his delivery:** Brace yourself—it looks like you have an early talker on your hands. It's still important to manage your expectations. Don't expect Baby to incisively critique your parenting skills right away. His insights will be limited by a small vocabulary, typically consisting of "dodo" and "umph." Once you factor in tone, however, you'd be surprised how withering those two words can be.

Stimulate the early talker with language games. Amuse her by

dangling a participle just out of the intended antecedent's reach. Toss her an innuendo to see if she can catch it. (Never, however, withhold exclamation marks even to make an important point.)

**If your child is more of a hisser:** This suggests he has accidentally mastered Parseltongue, the dialect Harry Potter uses to converse with snakes. If this happens to your baby, the onus is on you to learn how to writhe fluidly across the kitchen floor, flicking your tongue in and out.

**If your infant is an interrogator:** Be prepared to answer hundreds of questions per day, ranging from "Why don't fish have eyebrows?" to "Why don't you go change into something more comfortable while I position myself in the boppy?"

**If your baby is a color commentator:** Certain miracles develop a strong compulsion to dissect local gymnastic competitions and bake sales in a hushed but ardent voice. Never interrupt Baby when she's on a roll unless you absolutely must go to a commercial break.

**If your offsping is a gossip:** Urge him to clarify which tidbits he's passing on are "confidential" and which are "*super*-confidential" so you can act accordingly.

**Other types of talker:** If you suspect that your miracle is turning out to be a double-talker, an auctioneer, a slam poet, a military informant, or an unctuous White House tour guide, contact your doctor immediately.

# Relatively Speaking

## THE PROGRESS OF AN EARLY TALKER VS. A LATE TALKER

| The Highly Verbal Samantha | | The More Taciturn Todd |
| --- | --- | --- |
| Coos in complex, multi-faceted ways that wow the pigeon community. | **0-3** months | Cries a little. Wonders why a little. Burps. |
| Babbles "stories" with a clear beginning and end, followed by a graceful denouement. | **3-6** months | Naps a great deal. Coughs twice. |
| Manages to say "baba" (bottle). Moves on quickly to "*baba ghanoush.*" | **6-9** months | Bonds with his new Tough Talkin' Teddy, yet fails to emulate this role model. |
| Forms two-word sentences such as "Hey, lady!" and "Vive France!" | **9-12** months | Remains largely silent, but begins to show real promise as a sushi chef. |
| Begins describing objects—too vividly, in Grandma's opinion | **1-2** years | Mutely invents a spicy tofu roll; ventures to Walden Pond to rethink priorities |
| Suddenly hits a developmental plateau. Panics. Struggles to find *le mot juste*— or even *le mot adequate.* | **2-2½** years | Stuns parents by suddenly reciting the lyrics to "Don't Stop Believin'" by Journey |
| Remains blocked. Replaces security blanket with security thesaurus. | **2½-3** years | Dictates self-help book, *The Seven Habits of Highly Effective Silent Starers.* |
| Slowly regains confidence. Shakily uses a pluperfect subjunctive clause while recounting her recent trauma. | **3-3½** years | As a fixture on the speaking circuit, makes light of his former muteness: "God! What was I thinking?!" |
| Commands a vocabulary of 40,000 words, including "hubris." | **4** years | Knows 40,001 words, including "That chatty Samantha chick's hot." |

# Rambling Poses
## INTERPRETING BABY'S BODY LANGUAGE

Even during that awkward period when their tongues don't work, miracles aren't really at a loss for words. They're simply speaking to you through their limbs and postures. Here's how to "read" five classic poses:

### I.
### The Time-Out Pose
*Averts eyes, twists away, folds in limbs.*

**Baby is saying:**
"I'm overstimulated and need some quiet time alone. I'm thinking mid-weekish. Oh, it doesn't matter . . . either Spain or Mexico. But not that little villa in Majorca. You know, with the mildew?"

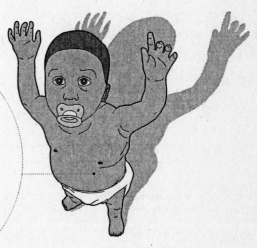

### 2.
### The "Hold Me" Pose
*Looks up at you, lifts arms.*

**Baby is saying:**
"Hey, what's going on? You look bored and unfulfilled. Would it help if you could cuddle me and walk around the room murmuring soothing things? Because if that's where you're at, it's completely doable. I have four minutes free . . ."

### 3.
### The Alert Readiness Pose
*Clasps hands cutely,*
*leans toward you, smiles.*

**Baby is saying:**
"Boy, am I glad you're back!
You'll *never* believe what's been going
on here! Did you know Nanny is totally
Wiccan? The minute you left,
all her friends came over to dance naked
around the fireplace and keen like
wolves, and then we sacrificed
Daddy's clownfish to the moon
goddess and . . .Hi!"

### 4.
### The C Pose
*As part of a sequence involving*
*the Y, M, and A Poses,*
*Baby forms theletter "C" with arms.*

**Baby is saying:**
"Daddy, what is this song? It's so . . .
anthemic. You seem to think it's
just a feel-good ditty, but it's obviously
laden with alternative-lifestyle
innuendoes. What's up
with that?"

### 5.
### The Evaluation Pose
*Steeples fingers,*
*purses lips, gazes at you intensely.*

**Baby is saying:**
"Are we absolutely sure
you're my biological parents?
Anyway, moving on . . . wow,
I'm hungry."

# Advanced Gesturing

## TAKING BODY TALK TO THE NEXT LEVEL

As expressive as body language is, its limited scope prevents your miracle from discussing his goals in truly concrete terms. Good news: Researchers have discovered that preverbal infants can learn to communicate extensively using coded gesture systems like the three popular methods shown here. Not only do these techniques speed the acquisition of real language, they allow Baby to mingle comfortably with simultaneous interpreters and melodramatic Japanese people.

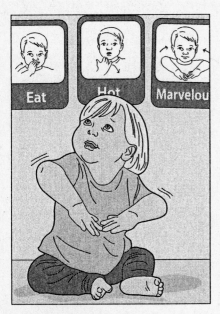

**1.**

### Sign Language

The easiest method: Each time you say a key word, show Baby the corresponding sign. Soon, he will be expressing important ideas himself such as "stop," "slow," and "253 kilometers to Berlin."
**Pros:** No consultant fees beyond an occasional $20 for the manicurist.
**Cons:** Sudden hand cramps can force Baby to pause—right in the middle of a suspenseful story about Daddy's apparently growing love for online gambling.

**2.**

### Kabuki Theater

Another great way to get your baby "talking" is to steep him in the ancient Kabuki tradition, a Japanese dramatic form that relies heavily on grunting, braying, scowling, and KISS makeup.
**Pros:** Gives Baby the opportunity to make a surprise trapdoor entrance while imparting universal truths about morality, heroism, and beauty.
**Cons:** Less useful for conveying specific truths like "I pooped."

**These popular non-verbal methods leave Baby with powerfully fidgety hands and a certain expertise when it comes to puffy wigs.**

**3.**

**Semaphore**

The best choice for rugged, outdoorsy miracles, this flag-signal system was originally designed to help eighteenth-century sailors communicate with each other across great distances.

**Pros:** Equips Baby to chat at length with nerdy naval historians.

**Cons:** Social Services may feel compelled to investigate reports that you're forcing a baby to communicate with you across great distances "using what appear to be napkins."

## A GLOSSARY OF PARENTESE

Your baby will learn to enunciate English even more quickly if you address him in the high-pitched, sing-song dialect known as "parentese." Some key words and phrases:

**Beddy-bye:** Time to retire.
**Blankie:** A blanket.
**Blankie statement:** Sweeping generalization. *Usage:* "Kendra, we don't make blankie statements when discussing race or gender."
**Boo-boo:** A minor wound.
**B-b-b-b-boo:** A minor speech impediment.
**Dada:** Male caregiver.
**Dadaism:** The male caregiver's tendency to make absurdist art when he should be bathing Baby.
**Din-din:** A meal taken in a cacophonous restaurant.
**Jammies:** Size 1 pajamas that have become mysteriously clogged in the upstairs toilet.
**Kitty:** A small cat.
**Mansiony:** A small home.
**Owie:** Term used to express sympathy (from the French, *Ah, oui!*)
**Pee-pee:** A legume.
**Tee-tee:** A golf neccessity.
**Uppie:** The desire to be lifted by a parent or a pharmaceutical.
**Wa-Wa:** Global conflict. As in "Wa-Wa I" or "Wa-Wa II."
**Wittle:** Small.
**Wittler:** Smaller, often handcarved.
**Wuv:** Ardent emotion.
**Wuv Hangover:** The painful consequences of too much wuv.

CRISIS MANAGEMENT

# Who's Crying Now?

WHEN FACED WITH A SOBBING BABY, IT'S TEMPTING TO SEEK RELATIONSHIP COUNSELING. PROCEED WITH CAUTION.

In a crisis, even babies with polished gesturing skills tend to communicate by crying their eyes out. Unfortunately, these disturbed infants sometimes decide to communicate both day and night for two weeks straight, leaving their poor parents struggling to interpret a torrent of information.

If this happens to you, first confirm that your child's physical needs are being met. Is he wet? Is he hungry? Does he crave a light loofahing? If you've satisfied all concerns and Baby continues to shriek, your next step is to systematically work your way through the various expert "no cry" strategies:

- Cuddle Baby.
- No, on second thought, shun Baby.
- Scrap that: Lovingly bind Baby's limbs.
- Cuddle her again but *this time really mean it.*

If nothing works, it may be time to sit down with your bawling infant and suggest couples therapy. He will likely balk at first, insisting with misplaced pride that he's

merely got a speck of dirt in his eye, but most perfect babies eventually agree.

Now comes the hardest part: Finding a competent, state-certified counselor to help you and your miracle resolve the underlying issues that have led to this stormy impasse. Even therapists with years of experience working with couples can fall short when it comes to resolving parent-baby conflicts. You'll know you've chosen poorly if:

1. **Your counselor provides too little structure for the session:** He allows Baby to interrupt your sobbing with her own wails and to shriek over your shrieking, then concludes the scheduled hour by smugly announcing, "Well, I think we've all gotten quite a bit off our chests."

2. **He resorts to diagnostic clichés:** It's ridiculous how many therapists insist that

Baby is just grieving the loss of her placenta.

3. **He fails to offer coping strategies:** A good therapist helps his clients improve their interactive dynamic—suggesting, for instance, that the next time your miracle weeps ceaselessly, instead of taking it personally, you calmly say, "What I'm *hearing* is that you feel like crying for the duration. Is that at all accurate?"

4. **He favors one of you over the other:** He says to Baby, "Why hang in there? Why be a victim? Move out!" or turns to you and shouts, "What do you see in this miracle? Can you really see a future here? Do you have any Extra-Strength Advil, by chance?!"

5. **He reveals that he is actually a salesman specializing in six-by-eight foot soundproofing panels:** And offers you a great deal with free installation.

## SLEEP TALKING

**If Baby still seems anguished post-treatment, try decoding his dreams for clues.**

Though scientists have long understood that infants dream more actively than adults, nobody knew what babies dreamt *about* until experts at Center for Sleep Theory in New York discovered exactly how to take a wild guess. The secret: Track the direction of your miracle's rapid eye movements as he sleeps.

**If Baby's eyeballs move from left to right:** He is likely dreaming about doing something horizontal—such as crawling rapidly away from you.

**If they move up and down:** He is likely dreaming of doing something vertical— such as rocketing into space to flee you.

**If Baby's eyes suddenly snap open:** He is likely wondering why you're not in bed when you're clearly suffering from sleep-deprivation-induced paranoia.

# Noun on a Hot Tin Roof

## A ONE-ACT PLAY IN WHICH TWO LOVING PARENTS EXPOSE THEIR MIRACLE TO LANGUAGE

**THE SCENE:** A family in a park. Countless objects have been labelled with Post-it Notes, including the body parts of "Mommy" (a focused, slightly weary woman) and "Daddy" (a rogue). Their baby, "Sasha," sits nearby, indifferent to the goings-on.

**Mommy:**
*[pointing]* Look, Sasha, a bird! Can you say "bird"?

**Daddy:**
It's a *newborn* bird!

**Mommy:**
Well, no, actually, it's a mature bird. Look, Sasha, a *wise old bird*.

*Sasha continues to study his fingers.*

**Daddy:**
It's a *brown* bird, that's for sure. Can you say "brown"?

**Mommy:**
Personally, I'd call that taupe. Sasha, can you stop saying "brown," and murmur "taupe" instead?

**Daddy:**
If you ask me, the bird is *dreary*. Mommy is *so sorry* she wasted your time.

**Mommy:**
*[to Daddy]* You're sitting on my Post-it Note.

**Daddy:**
Which one?

**Mommy:**
"Left thigh."

**Daddy:**
*[retrieves Post-it]* I don't know . . . do we really want to draw his attention to your left thigh right now? We agreed not to disturb him . . .

*Sasha stares contentedly at his thumb.*

**Mommy:**
*[gives Daddy a slow burn, then recalls her duties]*
Look, Sasha, a *tree!*

**Daddy:**
That's a *red oak tree!* Can you say "red"?

**Mommy:**
Actually, it's a *dwarf oak tree.*
Look, Sasha, characteristically tiny leaves!

**Daddy:**
Mommy is sorry she showed you a stunted tree, Baby.

**Mommy:**
No, Mommy is not!

**Daddy:**
Can you say "sad, stunted tree," Sasha? Can you say "hurtful metaphor for developmental sluggishness"?

*Sasha sneezes as Mommy dissolves into tears and Daddy rolls eyes.*

**Mommy:**
*[still sniffling, pointing up]* Look, Sasha, is that the *sky?*

**Daddy:**
The sky is *blue.* Blue is a *color.*

**Mommy:**
And it's also a mood. Sometimes known as *postpartum depression.*

**Daddy:**
Not in our house. We call it *silly self-indulgence.*

**Mommy:**
*[pointing at Daddy]* Look at the *lout,* Sasha! *L-O-U-T!*

**Daddy:**
*Lout* is another word for *fantastic!*

*Sasha abruptly raises his head . . .*

**Sasha:**
Since when?

*Both parents are stunned into silence.*

**Sasha:**
*[crawling over to his mother]* I love you, Mommy, even if you have a temporary serotonin imbalance and are uptight about naming objects accurately. Can you say "anal-retentive"?

**Mommy:**
*[dazedly]* Anal-retentive.

**Sasha:**
*[turning to his father]* And I love you, Daddy, even when you're passive-aggressive and fail to appreciate Mommy's superhuman efforts to lose the baby weight.

**Daddy:**
*[to Sasha]* Don't I get to say any words?

**Sasha:**
Okay, Daddy. You can say "the end."

**Daddy:**
The end.

# Baby's First Word

## HELPING HIM COPE WITH SOCIETAL PRESSURES TO MAKE IT A GOOD ONE

It's no wonder certain perfect babies are a bit tongue-tied initially. Given the way some parents react if their child's first word isn't impressive enough to wow family and friends, you'd be hesitant, too.

We've all heard the story about the couple who claimed their miracle's debut word was "pineapple," when it was really just "tee-tee," a crude approximation of "tinsel." Or the parents who doctored a video of their child yawning so that she appears to be enunciating "Piccadilly" in clear, bell-like tones.

It wasn't always this way. As recently as the sixties, a classic word like "mama" sufficed, but expectations soon rose. Seventies parents began coaxing exotic utterances like "om" and "muesli" from their babies, while the most talked-about eighties infants were those who spontaneously spouted BMW model names like "635CSi." After a brief early nineties trend for stark statements like "ick" and "nil," the current preference for longer, more demanding words emerged.

As an enlightened parent, you'll want to shield Baby from this madness so that her first verbal fumblings are as stress-free as possible:

- **Create a supportive environment:** Resist the temptation to plaster Baby's nursery with posters like, "How About 'Innocuous'?" or "Consider 'Hippopotamus.'"
- **Offer Baby a handicap:** Make it clear that, if she is in any way dissatisfied with her first effort, you'll agree to discard it.
- **Encourage the spirit of Norman Mailer to briefly inhabit your child:** This practically guarantees that Baby will deliver a memorable, if slightly pompous, word.

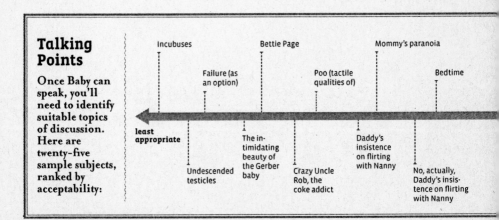

**Talking Points**

Once Baby can speak, you'll need to identify suitable topics of discussion. Here are twenty-five sample subjects, ranked by acceptability:

least appropriate

Incubuses

Failure (as an option)

Bettie Page

Poo (tactile qualities of)

Mommy's paranoia

Bedtime

Undescended testicles

The intimidating beauty of the Gerber baby

Crazy Uncle Rob, the coke addict

Daddy's insistence on flirting with Nanny

No, actually, Daddy's insistence on flirting with Nanny

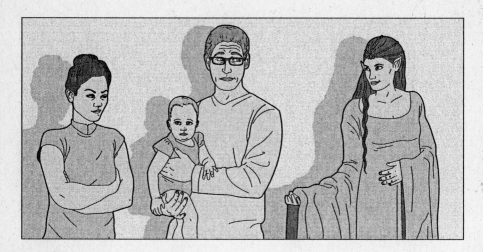

# CHOOSING A FOREIGN-LANGUAGE NANNY

**English is fun, but if Baby wants to make a killing in the global markets, he'll need to learn another language fast. One solution: Hire a nanny of foreign extraction to conspire with Baby in her native tongue. Which dialect is best? It all depends on your child's long-term career goals:**

**Mandarin:** Ideal for babies who've shown at least some interest in world domination.
**Arabic:** Increasingly crucial for budding crisis negotiators.

**Spanish:** Perfect for infants with potential to import premium coffee.
**French:** Best for scornful tots with a grudging interest in cheesemongering.

**Russian:** A great option for complex, brooding babies who might flourish in the Moscow mafia.
**Welsh:** Will surely be useful for something or other . . .

**Elvish:** Only recommended if Baby is determined to unlock the secrets of Middle Earth.
**Canadian:** Virtually useless outside of Canada. Avoid.

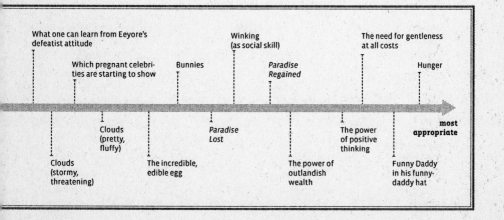

# Advance Warnings
## HOW TO READ YOUR BABY'S THOUGHTS BY
## SCRUTINIZING HER OBSESSIVELY

R aising the bar for parental sensitivity, some couples have begun to use "elimination communication," a traditional Third-World method, to anticipate their infant's bowel movements. The second they notice Baby scowling in a certain squirmy way, they rush him to the potty. Removing the need for diapers, this wonderful system asks only that you gaze at Baby continuously, even while driving off a slight cliff. Of course, "poo face" is just one of several similar early-warning signs. Here's a guide to ten more:

| Warning | Signal | Translation |
| --- | --- | --- |
| *Procrastination* communication | Baby squirms, holds up one finger | Baby needs to poo, but would rather cry for 20 minutes first. |
| *Disembarkation* communication | Stares meaningfully at the floor | Has had enough of Daddy's horsey ride for now, thanks. |
| *Fragmentation* communication | Crosses and uncrosses eyes | Giving some thought to developing multiple personalities. |
| *Liquidation* communication | Starts babbling aggressively | On the verge of selling toys for 70% less than warehouse prices. |
| *Appalachian* communication | Scratches ass, runs amok | Wouldn't mind a less structured, more hillbilly existence. |
| *Gentrification* communication | Measures walls | Getting ready to pick up a few crown moldings at Home Depot. |
| *Inside-information* communication | Tingles visibly | Feels a stock tip coming on. |
| *Standing-ovation* communication | Springs to feet | About to applaud an unusually brave Oscar acceptance speech. |
| *Renunciation* communication | Frowns slightly, falteringly | Preparing to give up title "Happiest Baby on the Block," feeling it's no longer accurate. |
| *Jubilation* communication | Corners of lips spontaneously curl up | Hold on . . . may have spoken too soon. |

# 10.

## The Perfect First
# BIRTHDAY

Congratulations! Your miracle has reached the pivotal age of one. This is clearly cause for ecstatic celebration, but remember: Perfect babies hate clichés. So resist the temptation to throw yours a predictably extravagant birthday party. No baby should suffer embarrassment just because his parents couldn't come up with anything more original than renting out the Astrodome and filling it with meerkats, palm trees, mylar balloons shaped like Thomas the Tank Engine, $1500 chocolate-milk fountains, imported fake snow for sledding, and high-maintenance trilingual clowns.

Restraint is key.

This doesn't mean your child's party should be dull. Within its sensible budget, it should still efficiently take guests' breath away. If you're having trouble developing creative concepts, take cues from your miracle. Is he a fretful child? Throw him a fretting festival. Is she the sort of infant who likes to sketch up ideas for housing complexes? Use a drafting table to serve an array of architecturally inspired refreshments.

In all matters, try to respect Baby's wishes. If he expresses the desire for an all-ice cube menu, go for it. You may be perceived as an incompetent parent with a poor grasp of nutrition, but after all, it is Baby's special day.

# Fête Accompli

## ACHIEVING THE PERFECT MIX OF INNOVATION AND RESTRAINT ISN'T EASY, BUT BABY MAY WELL NOTICE YOUR EFFORTS

For Helene and Bob Fischer of Atlanta, a winning party started with a winning theme. Rejecting their first choice, "Crown Princesses of Europe," as too snooty, they eventually settled on "Flawlessness as Embodied by the Color White." Once Agnes, their daughter, okayed this key decision, all the pieces of their modest but inventive party fell into place:

1. **Living decorations:** Rather than hang expensive streamers, the Fischers invited exotic white birds to perch nearby, aiming for a casual party mix of cockatoos and egrets. Cost: $0.

2. **A simple, practical dress code:** Guests were politely asked to dress in "unblemished white separates" and to bring a fresh change of clothing in case of blemishes.

3. **Focused gift bags:** Instead of overwhelming Baby's friends with random trinkets, the Fischers chose surefire treats: a collector's photo of Agnes, sugar-free gummy bears, and a video of Agnes sleeping.

4. **Cake options:** To limit fuss, they ordered a trio of white number-one cakes in different fonts in case Agnes was feeling particularly Helvetica that day or suddenly craved serifs.

5. **Baby's favorite snacks:** To give their daughter a sense of ownership, they let her select the hors d'oeuvres. As original as ever, Agnes went for raw turnip, StoveTop stuffing, seaweed, and Kleenex.

6. **A diverting craft activity:** The Fischers decided it would be fun to let guests chisel a statue of Agnes from a block of Italian marble they had kicking around.

7. **Strict present guidelines:** In the interest of reducing waste, the invitation specified: "No plastic gifts! No helicopters! Only rare vintage toys or FCS-certified wood." Most guests happily complied.

8. **A reasonably priced "character" entertainer:** Babies love interacting with actors dressed up as Big Bird or Dora the Explorer in colorful plush costumes. The Fischers opted for "Emily Dickinson" from the surprisingly affordable "Reclusive Poets" category.

9. **Homespun entertainment:** Agnes embraced the chance to demolish an angel-shaped piñata while accompanying herself on piano.

10. **A touch of livestock:** You certainly don't need an entire petting zoo, but a farm animal adds warmth. The Fischers arranged to have one perfect llama hang-glide in on cue.

# Memoirs of a Miracle

### BABIES RECALL THEIR
### FAVORITE FIRST-BIRTHDAY MOMENTS

"I vaguely remember Daddy renting an inflatable bounce-house. A late-Victorian model with lovely gables. So that was fun."
—*Tabitha Grace Spitz, age 7*

"Sorry, I'm drawing a blank. Maybe a life-sized dolphin cake?"
—*Agnew P. Hernandez, age 5*

"My birthday's in December and Mommy came up with this great theme, 'Winter One-derland.' But then the lady next door threw a 'Winter *Two*-derland' party for her twins, totally stealing mommy's thunder."
—*Holiday Spirit McKenzie, age 7*

"Screeching . . . so much screeching . . ."
—*Matthew D. Frith, age 4*

"I actually thought the Little Mermaid was going to come—like, swim up in a torrent of seawater or whatever. But she just showed up on foot and played a banjo for $300."
—*Anika Eloise Tremblay, age 10*

"There's a photo of me dancing the Limbo expertly, but I think it was Photoshopped."
—*Panther Gottlieb, age 4*

"It was a queer, sultry summer, the summer they electrocuted the Rosenbergs, and I didn't know what I was doing in New York. Oh sorry, that's the first line of *The Bell Jar*."
—*Harmonica Johnson, age 14*

"Let's just say I loved every last hour of it."
—*Tilda Kinkaid, age 3*

"It's all a blur, but apparently my dad—who's really down on consumerism—persuaded the guests' parents to observe his no-gifts policy by buying them all new cars."
—*Randolph Chan, age 9*

"'Tulips. No, hold on, peonies? Narcissi?"
—*Peter Wachowich, age 5*

"I asked Mom to describe my party, but she just said, 'Honey, you really had to be there.'"
—*Lisbon Brown, age 7*

## CROWNING GLORIES

**A distinctive party hat can make your miracle feel extra-special on his birthday. Shop carefully, however: Some models are dangerously regal.**

**UNSAFE**
This bulky hat—based on the legendary Russian imperial crown—can strain Baby's neck and trigger dominant behavior.

**SAFE**
This lightweight topper—inspired by Napoleon's gold laurel wreath—can also trigger dominant behavior, but in a fully ergonomic way.

**MULTI-TASKING**

# Educational Soirees

AMBITIOUS PARENTS WHO WANT
TO MAXIMIZE BABY'S LEISURE TIME MAY PREFER ONE
OF THESE MORE FOCUSED OPTIONS.

| "Discovering Art" Party | "Eco-Awareness" Party | "Office Politics" Party |
|---|---|---|
| Exposes infants to key visual concepts and the current market for 20th Century American lithographs. | A stark event designed to wake infants up to the devastating horrors that are facing our planet. | A tightly scheduled fête that equips babies with all the tactics they need to navigate the corporate jungle. |
| **Decor:** None. Babies must learn, sooner or later, that no one takes decorative art seriously. | **Decor:** A unique centerpiece created by stacking fifty disposable diapers into an artful pile of landfill. | **Decor:** "For Better or For Worse" cartoons—quickly replaced by framed prints more worthy of rising stars. |
| **Refreshments:** A "cake" that, on inspection, is merely dabs of colorful icing, bringing the techniques of Impressionism to life. | **Refreshments:** A butterless cake. ("We just felt it was important not to use products from methane-farting cows.") | **Refreshments:** Babies are given an expense account and strict instructions to be back in one hour with laughably implausible receipts. |
| **Entertainment:** A Sotheby's representative in a Tigger costume auctions off a lesser Jackson Pollack. | **Entertainment:** A sad clown leads the babies in an upbeat sing-along about the tragedy of deforestation. | **Entertainment:** A mime wears an inappropriate turtleneck to a "job interview"; another mime cuts the interview short. |
| **Activity:** Babies are taught to hold wine glasses gingerly while dismissing Andy Warhol's later work. | **Activity:** Babies are urged to smash a jumbo-jet-shaped piñata, releasing a festive cascade of "pollution." | **Activity:** Babies are ushered into a conference room and encouraged to curry favor with each other. |
| **Gift bag Contents:** A charcoal eraser and a guide to two-point perspective. | **Gift bag contents:** A small solar panel and some beautifully recycled tin. | **Gift bag contents:** A lollipop and a mostly positive performance appraisal. |

# "Here's To Baby!"

## DELIVERING THE BIRTHDAY TOAST

I t's easy to get nervous when the time comes to raise a glass to your perfect baby. How can any proud parent sum up a growing miracle's charm and achievements in just a few snappy anecdotes? Here are a few useful guidelines:

**I.**

**Allow yourself twenty snappy anecdotes:** You can hardly skip over key moments like Baby's first smile. Or his second smile, which was arguably cuter. Cut your comments short, however, if Baby gives you the "wrap it up" signal.

**2.**

**Focus on the positive:** While you'll want to highlight your miracle's love for his antigravity chamber (see page TK), you needn't mention the time he accidentally got locked inside it—unless Baby thinks it'll get a laugh.

**3.**

**Try not to cry:** This may be difficult if Baby starts crying first. Or even shrieking. After that, it's pretty tough to resist.